Will the Gig Economy Prevail?

The Future of Capitalism series

Colin Crouch

———

Will the Gig Economy Prevail?

polity

First published in 2019 by Polity Press

Polity Press
65 Bridge Street
Cambridge CB2 1UR, UK

Polity Press
101 Station Landing
Suite 300
Medford, MA 02155, USA

ISBN-13: 978-1-5095-3243-8
ISBN-13: 978-1-5095-3244-5 (pb)

A catalogue record for this book is available from the British Library.

Typeset in 11 on 15 Sabon by
Servis Filmsetting Ltd, Stockport, Cheshire
Printed and bound in the United Kingdom by Clays Ltd, ElcograFph S.p.A.

For further information on Polity, visit our website:
politybooks.com

For Joan

Contents

Acknowledgements

I am grateful to Joan Crouch for help with the whole text, and to Mark Freedland for passages of legal interpretation. Neither share responsibility for any defects in the final product.

Abbreviations

ALMP	active labour market policy
AT	Austria
AU	Australia
BE	Belgium
CA	Canada
CEE	Central and Eastern Europe
CH	Switzerland
CZ	Czechia
DE	Germany
DK	Denmark
EL	Greece
ES	Spain
FI	Finland
FR	France
HU	Hungary
IE	Ireland
IL	Israel

Abbreviations

IT	Italy
JA	Japan
KO	Korea
MX	Mexico
NL	Netherlands
NO	Norway
NZ	New Zealand
OECD	Organisation for Economic Cooperation and Development
PL	Poland
PT	Portugal
SE	Sweden
SK	Slovakia
TR	Turkey
TWA	temporary work agency
UK	United Kingdom
US	United States of America

1

The Rise of Precarious Work

The death in January 2018 of a courier working in southern England for the German logistics firm DPD attracted unwelcome attention to the dark side of what has become known as the 'gig economy'. The courier was not an employee of DPD, but for nineteen years had been a self-employed contractor to the firm. His death had been caused by a deteriorating diabetes condition, for which he had missed several hospital appointments. This followed a day when DPD had fined him £150 because, as a result of attending an appointment, he had failed to deliver his allocation of parcels for the day. In the wake of the furore surrounding his death, DPD changed its policy on workers' medical appointments, but deeper questions remain surrounding the idea of workers who are not employees of a firm and for whom the firm accepts no employer responsibilities, but who can be disciplined by that firm. That is the idea at the heart of the gig economy.

The issue is not a marginal one. The gig economy is seen by many neoliberal policy-makers as an ideal form of work, set gradually to replace the costly rigidities of the old-fashioned employment contract. Firms can maximize flexibility by calling on and paying self-employed workers only when they need them to perform specific tasks, avoiding the social insurance charges, minimum wage obligations and the host of other responsibilities that come with so-called standard employment. Workers can enjoy the freedom of being entrepreneurs, working when they like and for whom they like. In a further response to the case of the diabetic courier, DPD offered its couriers a choice. They could become normal employees, with rights to sick pay, paid holidays and a pension, but being paid a lower rate for their deliveries. This gives workers that ultimate prize of the capitalist economy: freedom of choice.

But are workers in economic circumstances so tight that they cannot risk taking time off for a hospital appointment likely to forego ready money now in order to guarantee sick pay and a pension at some future time? More generally, can a person who works full time for one firm be said to have the freedom of the self-employed? And how can a firm that engages thousands of people as couriers not be their employer? The emerging new world of flexible working arrangements is replete with verbal and legal tricks of this kind. Corporations such as the giant taxi firm Uber, which organize their work over the Internet, claim to be mere 'platforms' and therefore outside any employment relationship. If they arrange their affairs skilfully, they can also claim not even to have a geographical location on this planet and therefore choose the fiscally most benign jurisdiction in which to report all their profits. Since the Internet constitutes all that is new and pioneering, anyone who criticizes their practices is accused of standing in the way of progress.

The term 'gig economy' is itself deceptive. It resonates with the shows or gigs organized for entertainers, who perform events at various locations, with no long-term commitment to the places or the groups organizing them. But these entertainers are genuinely self-employed; they are in a true free market, working for several different organizations and dependent on no individual one. This is very different from the situation of people engaged in making deliveries day in, day out, for one or two large corporations on which they are almost totally dependent for making a living, and which may well stipulate their hours of work. The description of this as a 'gig' seems more like a cynical attempt to associate a problematic form of employment with the romance of the entertainment business than a genuine attempt to define a new form of work relationship.

It is even highly doubtful that the gig is as important as its effusive advocates claim (see, for example, Annabel Denham's [2018] 'The Gig [*sic*] economy is the future and women can lead the charge'). The Brookings Institution estimated that, although gig work was certainly growing fast (between 2010 and 2014, 'non-employer' [i.e., gig] firms offering taxi services in large US cities grew by 69 per cent against 17 per cent among firms with employees), such firms accounted for only 3 per cent of total US business revenue (Hathaway and Muro 2016). Research by the McKinsey Global Institute (2016) claimed that up to 162 million people, or 20 to 30 per cent of the total workforce, across Europe and the US were engaged in 'independent work'. Although McKinsey included the phrase 'gig economy' in their report's title, independent work is a far more extensive category, also covering self-employed persons as normally understood. The figure still seems high, given the general historical decline that has been taking place in self-employment in advanced economies, with only Greece and Spain having proportions like those suggested by McKinsey. There must be some overlap here with the shadow (i.e., illegal) economy, all of whose workers will lack employee status. Also, McKinsey found that about 40 per cent of independent workers were 'casual' – that is, not having their work as a major component of their life activities – mainly students, retired people and others who would not be counted as part of the total workforce in official statistics. These groups combined could bring us closer to the McKinsey estimate, but students and retired people doing odd jobs do not presage a new age of entrepreneurs liberated from having regular jobs.

McKinsey also distinguished among 30 per cent of all independent workers who were 'free agents', voluntarily having such employment as their main work activity, 14 per cent who were 'reluctantly' in this category, and would have preferred to find dependent employment, and 16 per cent who were doing such work only because they were 'financially strapped'. It is not possible to determine from McKinsey's data the proportions of contented workers in the gig economy. It is, however, clear that such work is not universally welcomed by those working in it. The Taylor Review, established by the UK government to examine working arrangements in the gig, and generally favourable towards the phenomenon, found that only 25 per cent of sixteen- to thirty-year-olds would consider working in it (Taylor 2016: 28). Using a slightly different approach, and coming from a more critical position, the European Foundation for the Study of Working Life found that 17 per cent of all formally self-employed workers in the European Union were 'vulnerable', in the sense that they worked for only one customer, while a further 8 per cent had little autonomy in practice (Eurofound 2015).

Further evidence of the small size of the gig will be presented in chapter 4 below. One can easily understand why its advocates want to talk it up and stress its exciting associations with the Internet, as it promises employers a combination otherwise impossible to achieve: workers who are completely subordinate to a firm's authority but for whom it has no responsibility.

But the gig is just one form taken by a far more extensive, general attempt by firms, neoliberal thinkers and public policy-makers to free employers of responsibilities to those who work for them while retaining if not intensifying the dependence of those workers on the firms. The appropriate term to describe the position of all such workers is 'precarious' (Freedland 2016). One form that is popular with employers is 'on-call' work or 'zero-hours' contracts, where employees are paid only for hours when the employer calls them in, though they have to stand ready and available to be called in at short notice and are often therefore unable to take on other work or indeed leisure activities. The Office for National Statistics (2017) estimated that around 900,000 people worked under such conditions in the United Kingdom, though 28 per cent of those involved were students. Slightly different are 'marginal' jobs, known in Germany as 'Minijobs' and 'Midijobs', where workers are offered work for only a small number of hours in a week and very low earnings, but enough to disqualify them from claiming unemployment benefits. Another form is the use of temporary contracts set to expire before workers acquire any rights. This is found mainly in countries where employees with permanent contracts enjoy extensive rights. It is therefore not so commonly used in countries like the UK or the US, where the rights of standard employees are in any case limited. Finally there is the shadow or illegal economy, where no legal contract exists at all.

It is often argued that the growth of this kind of employment is producing a 'dualism' in labour markets, with a division between those who benefit from the full security of standard employment and those left in precariousness. There is truth in this, and we shall further examine it below (chapter 4), but it is partly yet another of the verbal tricks being played in the current politics of labour issues, as it enables ordinary standard employees, moderately or poorly paid, to be stigmatized as 'privileged', with the precarious being encouraged to see them as their enemies. Morandini (2017) has shown that, at least in Italy, labour market deregulation is supported not only by managers but also by precarious workers and the unemployed. However, in most advanced economies the rights of standard employees themselves have been steadily eroded. Growing insecurity is becoming a general condition for working people. Many occupations require considerable skill, employers usually want to retain skilled workers, and standard employment contracts are a useful means for doing this. But the people in what Standing (2009, 2011) calls the 'precariat' have no professionalism or occupational standards because no one bothers to equip them with skills or even experience. Firms are likely to dismiss them before they acquire the experience that entitles them to job upgrading (Lichtenstein 2010). They never acquire entitlement to such rights as maternity leave. Immigrants are particularly likely to be found among their number, often lacking basic citizenship rights and even elementary knowledge of rights.

The issues raised by the gig economy therefore extend beyond the problems of couriers, taxi drivers and cyclists delivering restaurant meals. They go to the heart of the changing relationship between those who use human labour and those who provide it, involve a wider range of precariousness than false self-employment, and have in no way left untouched the position of standard employees. The aim of this book is to explore the extent and range of different kinds of precariousness, to explain their rise and importance, and to propose changes in the way labour markets are governed. We need new ways of providing ordinary working people with security and predictability in their lives and of enabling them to acquire skills to adapt to a changing economy and technologies. This is in no way hostile to ideas of flexibility, innovation and entrepreneurship. As William Beveridge observed when he produced his plan for social security and a welfare state during the Second World War (Beveridge 1942), it is only if they have a base of security that people can be expected to welcome and collaborate in change.

The short answer that this book will give to the question in its title is: no, the gig economy will not become a paradigm form for work relations in the digitalized economy of the future. On the other hand, firms can get much of what they achieve with the gig through other forms of precariousness and by lobbying successfully for the dismantling of the security of standard employment.

Behind all these issues stands the ambiguous nature of the employment contract. While at one level it is an equal arrangement between two contracting parties, at another it prescribes an unequal relationship of authority. The main reason why the gig has acquired a prominence not justified by its actual importance is that it completely conceals the latter behind the former. The following chapter traces this ambiguity and how various contending parties have tried to come to terms with it. For much of the twentieth century a key development was the idea that the asymmetry of the relationship could be reduced if employees had certain rights against their employers. This led to the idea of standard employment, its contract enriched with various rights. During the neoliberal period, however, many employer spokespersons and their political allies have argued that employee rights simply constitute a constraint on business efficiency and should therefore be reduced. They have had considerable but by no means total success with this contention.

The Rise of Precarious Work

The current state of the conflict is reflected in recent changes in standard employment. It will be traced in chapter 3, mainly by examining statistics from most advanced industrialized economies. Chapter 4 will use the same approach to survey the growth or otherwise of the main forms of precarious work and to explore whether we are today witnessing a dualization of the labour market, separating an ever smaller secure core of largely older workers from a growing precarious workforce. Finally, chapter 5 makes some proposals for reforming work arrangements, designed to reduce the proportion of jobs that are precarious and to improve the quality of labour market regulation. The main proposal is for a reform of social insurance, making it a tax on the use of labour rather than on acceptance of responsibility as an employer.

2

Ambiguities of the Employment Contract

A contract implies two partners, equally free to enter into the arrangement or not, in principle equally well informed about its terms and able to contribute to making them. But the contract of employment differs from most others, in that one party, the employee, undertakes to place him- or herself under the authority and general disposal of the other, the employer. Once the contract has been made the relationship becomes highly unequal. Employment contracts are necessarily asymmetrical.

The asymmetry does not stop there. An employer is very frequently a large organization, while an employee is always an individual. In such cases, the former approaches contract-making with the assistance of legally qualified staff, expert in framing contracts favourable to the employer. Although the contract is seen in law as jointly owned by both parties, in reality it belongs to the employer, with the employee usually contributing nothing beyond a signature of acceptance. The employee's inferior position is matched by that of the great majority of individual customers of large enterprises, deemed to have accepted the producer's unilaterally determined and non-negotiable small-print contract terms by the mere act of purchasing the goods or services involved. The reality of life in societies characterized by large organizations, private or public, is that these set the terms of their relationships with ordinary individuals, whether customers, workers or small-scale suppliers, whose contract role is passive.

Labour law – a body of law distinct from contract law as such – has long recognized the problem of asymmetry (Freedland 2016; Verhulp 2008). Employees are granted certain rights – for example, to protection against unsafe and unhealthy conditions; against very long working hours; to compensation in case of loss of employment for no fault of their own; to paid holidays; in recent years to safeguard employment during times off for maternity or the obligations of parenthood; and to protection against various types of discrimination and prejudice. Legislation and courts have also recognized the right of employees to be represented by autonomous organizations, trade unions, which are able to offset some of the disadvantages of the imbalance of power in the contract. Of course, these rights exist within a general frame of law that enables employers to own and control property and assert authority over workers. Indeed, labour law also often defines the obligations owed by employees to employers, going beyond those in contract law as such (Freedland and Countouris 2008).

The reduced asymmetry of modern labour law did not come about easily. In English law employment was – and to some extent still is – governed by the ancient concept of 'master and servant', implying a relationship of personal subordination with an accompanying obligation of total loyalty on the part of the employee. The German idea of the employer as *Herr im Haus* – master in the house – also has overtones of domestic service, as do similar concepts in Italian law (Freedland and Countouris 2008: 59). Considerable struggle by trade unions and social reformers rather than a benign spread of enlightened views was necessary to achieve a shift from this position to one where the employer's authority was made constitutional – that is, subject to externally imposed constraints (Baccaro and Howell 2017; Emmenegger 2014; Korpi 1983).

Advocates of the gig economy present it as

giving equal freedom to platform companies and workers alike. They speak as though the gig turns the employment relationship into a truly equal contract, one shorn of the hierarchical implications of the employment relationship and therefore not requiring the balancing provisions of labour law to protect workers. But much of the asymmetry continues. True, gig workers can often choose their hours of work, both when and how many. However, the firms can also decide to accept on to their lists only those prepared to work for certain numbers of hours and at certain times of day. There is also no equivalent gain on the workers' side to match the firms' avoidance of all employer obligations, such as those for pensions, safety and maternity leave. On the other hand, this freedom from obligations, a pure example of the neoliberal model of the unregulated firm, is reaching limits. There have been cases of drivers working for Uber sexually assaulting female customers, bringing the firm under pressure to vet the persons it allows on to its lists. Every step of this kind makes the relationship more like one of employer and employee, with all its asymmetry.

At what point is this line crossed? English law courts have used a very restrictive test, favourable to the platform companies, determining that no employment relationship exists if a worker can substitute another person to perform the work. This puts platform jobs into the category of self-employment, but it does not correspond to normal understandings of that concept. The typical self-employed person works for a number of customers. In the best case, the worker can risk losing any one customer without the business collapsing; that is indeed a definitional criterion for being in a true market. But platform workers are often dependent on one, perhaps two, firms for all their employment. This is especially the case in sectors where a small number of firms dominate the market or where they require a high minimum number of hours.

English law is particularly complex in this area, since the Employment Rights Act 1996 (Section 230) defined a status of 'worker', coming between that of an employee and a self-employed person, and prescribed certain rights that had to be respected by those engaging a 'worker's' labour: the statutory minimum wage; protection against unlawful deductions from pay and against discrimination, including discrimination against part-time workers; and in some circumstances rights to sick pay and parental leave. Recent court cases in the UK suggest that at least some platform workers dependent on one or two enterprises for their supply of work are covered by one of the definitions of a 'worker' (the so-called 'limb b') in section 230(3) of the Act. Most notable was a decision of the Supreme Court in the case of Pimlico Plumbers ([2018] UKSC 29), which ruled that the substitutability test was not absolute. The judgements involved have been fine ones, dependent on the precise terms of a gig worker's engagement, and some platform firms have been settling cases out of court without acceptance of liability in order to avoid firm judicial rulings. In any case, 'workers' remain in the 'self-employed' category for tax and social security purposes, and are excluded from some important employment rights such as that not to be unfairly dismissed. The area remains one of considerable uncertainty.

Similar developments are occurring in the US. In 2015 the California Labor Commissioner's Office dealt with a complaint on behalf of Uber drivers, by arguing that the crucial point was who con-trolled workplace behaviour (Steinmetz 2015) – an approach favoured in the UK by the Taylor Review (Taylor 2016). However, in order to avoid class actions by its drivers in California and Massachusetts to test that proposition, Uber reached an out-of-court settlement, making certain concessions but insisting on continuing self-employed status. In cities around the world conflict continues around Uber and similar services, with local authorities seeking to regulate and firms either trying to avoid regulation by reaching ad hoc compromises or contesting authorities' right to regulate.

A fuller approach is that taken by Jeremias Prassl, who proposes that law should focus on the attributes of the provider of work, not the worker (Prassl 2018; Prassl and Risak 2016). A work provider should be considered an employer if it has the power to initiate and terminate the relationship; receives labour and its fruits; provides the work and the pay; and manages the market both within and outside the enterprise. Much platform work would be covered by such a definition.

Prassl is not among those commentators who are wholly hostile to the gig economy. He sees the value of new possibilities in work organization other than standard employment, particularly those that might help people get started in running their own firms. However, for an individual to be satisfied working in the gig implies their seeing a positive trade-off between gaining a certain amount of independence, and perhaps the capacity to use that position as a stepping stone to founding a small business of their own (depending on the obligations imposed by the non-employer), against loss of employment protection, interest representation and all but minimal social security. It should be assumed that the supply of such persons will be limited, and that beyond a certain level the gig will depend on more of those people whom McKinsey found to be 'reluctant' or 'cash-strapped'. There will also be certain demographic limitations on the supply of willing participants in the gig economy. It is not a kind of work that is useful as the main job for people raising a family or buying a home, or even renting a home of any size.

Overall, it must be assumed that the independence/security trade-off of the gig will not be very attractive. It is likely to flourish most where labour markets are slack, with surpluses of labour. This enables us to anticipate future developments in the sector. If labour shortages appear, or if firms acquire a need for more continuing commitment from their workforces, the balance of power will shift towards workers. Firms will start to offer employment-like security guarantees, and may even find that the trade-off they face between cost savings and workforce reliability tips the scales against remaining in the gig. There are already indications of this happening. Uber and Lyft are said to be considering being listed on the US stock exchange, but there is concern that investors will be discouraged by the instability of a self-employed workforce. In an attempt to recruit more drivers, Lyft has begun already to offer various fringe benefits. When the platform first developed, there would have been a pent-up stock of people eager (or desperate) to enter its employment: students with heavy loans, people who liked the idea of self-employment but were worried at the prospect of starting their own business, the unemployed. As this stock becomes a flow, its size should be expected to decline.

On the other hand, employers' demand for gig conditions with minimal security might be expected to grow, as information technology and artificial intelligence enable more and more work activities customarily performed on an employer's premises to be carried out in workers' own homes. Already many employers and employees make use of teleworking, whereby on some days an employee takes work home to do, perhaps when a child is sick or when some evening work is needed to meet a deadline after the offices have closed. Many of these activities could be carried out entirely at home, with electronic discussions, work delivery and monitoring. One thinks immediately of accounting, legal, ticketing and many other back-office tasks, as well as call centre and cold calling activities, but the development of three-dimensional printing would enable extension to certain manufacturing tasks too, given postal delivery of materials and a 3-D printer. As more firms discover the possibilities presented by digital platforms, the supply of such jobs may well outrun demand for them, leading to improvements in working conditions. The future is very open.

The historical development of standard employment

It is central to arguments in favour of the gig that it represents the cutting edge of modernity, as it uses information technology platforms, and that therefore all opposition to it derives from hostility to progress. When the UK government established the Taylor Review to examine problems in the gig, it contributed to this lustre, officially describing the phenomenon as 'emerging business practices' in 'the modern economy' (Taylor 2016). However, these practices also represent a return to far older forms of work organization. In parts of the clothing sector in the early stages of English industrialization, and more recently in China and other developing economies, firms made use of the 'putting out system'. The entrepreneur or his agent delivered quantities of cloth to workers, usually women, in their homes, where they had clothes-making machinery. Every so often the agent returned, collected the finished pieces and (if the work was judged satisfactory) paid for them. The women were not employees of the firm and were responsible for maintaining, heating and lighting their own work environment, and for its health and safety. While formally free from employment obligations, they were completely subordinate to the discipline of their non-employer, who could stipulate quality and quantity of production if payment were to be made and the work relationship maintained.

As now with the gig, from the entrepreneur's perspective this was an ideal way of using labour. Also like the gig, however, it came against certain limitations. If an activity required large numbers of persons to be brought together for the production tasks or for their adequate monitoring and control, factories, construction sites, offices and other work premises became necessary. As individuals' contributions to work tasks become integrated into tight webs of cooperation and use of complex machinery, the kind of control that could be achieved over a self-employed person solely responsible for producing individual items became inadequate. The idea of the employee, based on the ancient concept of master and servant and thus defined by a relationship of obedience to managerial authority, became highly useful.

Ambiguities of the Employment Contract

Nevertheless, the advantages to capitalists of the factory system were always double-edged. Gradually it became impossible to resist taking responsibility for the health and safety of the people whom they brought together in buildings under their control. Also, when workers came together in large numbers, they would begin to appreciate that they had some joint interests and try to form organizations to press these – trade unions. Employers and governments associated with them tried for a long time to suppress such developments. However, especially as struggles for extensions of the suffrage to working people became successful, it became impossible to prevent the growth of unions and a need to recognize them. Many employers even saw advantages in working with unions to regulate pay and working conditions in their enterprises. Meanwhile, political debate began to rage around other aspects of the employment relationship. Should workers have rights of notice, compensation, the receipt of stated reasons, if their employer wished to dispense with their services? Should they be supported at some level of living if they were prevented from working by the lack of employment, old age, accident, poor health or disability? And should employers be responsible for contributing to such support through systems of what became known as social insurance?

Ambiguities of the Employment Contract

In sectors such as docks and building sites, employers continued to make use of self-employed persons or employees on very casual contracts, hiring them for a few days or hours at a time with no ongoing commitment. While unions had long campaigned against such conditions, in the UK it finally became necessary to give full legal meaning to the concept of what we now call standard employment only after 1945, when the social insurance system was reformed to include all employees. The system, which was a genuinely insurance-based one, could not accept the burden of workers in casual employment. A definition of entitled employees was therefore developed that excluded those on casual forms of contract – an important example of what some Dutch scholars have called the contract of employment as an 'exclusionary device' (Knegt 2008a; Verhulp 2008). Meanwhile, however, the Labour government of the day was embarked on an eventually successful campaign to 'decasualize' work in the docks and elsewhere, putting most workers on to secure employment contracts. Casual labour was associated with poverty, deep insecurity and generally unstable lives (Whiteside 2017), and reducing it to a minimum was seen as a desirable goal. It is interesting to contrast that with the approach taken seventy years later by the Taylor Review, which, while calling for some limited rights for casual workers, argued that it was important that policy should '*reflect* the increasing casualization of the labour market' (Taylor 2016: 35; emphasis added).

The enrichment of standard employment and the neoliberal challenge

Standard employment, embodying the idea of full-time, non-temporary jobs with employment contracts, became established as a norm in most of today's advanced economies by the first half of the twentieth century. In subsequent decades the rights associated with employee status developed further. We can call this a movement from 'minimal' to 'enriched' standard employment. Some basic rights can be dated to the period of reforms that followed the Second World War, though only in Belgium and France was there job protection as such. Rights to join unions and sometimes obligations on employers to recognize them were more widespread. Especially in Germany and Austria, and to a limited extent also in Belgium, France, Italy and the Netherlands, employees could elect statutory representative committees with which employers were required at least to hold consultations. These mechanisms all reduced the asymmetry of the employment contract, if often in only minor ways.

Ambiguities of the Employment Contract

Major steps in the enrichment of standard employment followed the waves of worker and student protests and strikes of the late 1960s and subsequent commodity price inflation crises of the 1970s. One outcome was a strengthening of the role of unions in responsible wage-setting in order to try to contain the inflationary spiral if wage rises were constantly to try to keep pace with initially exogenous price rises. Another was an increase in workers' rights. Throughout Western Europe and Japan (but not in the US or, for different reasons, the Soviet bloc) they acquired legal protection against dismissal unless they had committed specified offences, as well as compensation or later re-employment in case of redundancy. A major innovation, which began in this period but which has strengthened and continued long into neoliberal turn against labour protection in general, was the introduction of rights for female employees before and after childbirth. Typically, mothers have been permitted to take periods of maternity leave with a guaranteed right to return to their positions. In some countries this later came to include rights to return at reduced numbers of hours, as well rights to parental leave (not always remunerated) for childcare purposes for both mothers and their partners. There has also been a growth in protection for the employment of disabled persons and rights to protection against discrimination on grounds of ethnicity or religion.

However, the seeds of an undermining of many of these achievements were being sown virtually simultaneously with such advances. The high inflation that had been an aspect of workers' and unions' power was leading many policy-makers to doubt the continued viability of the guarantee of full employment. If this target were removed from the core objectives of economic policy and replaced by the pursuit of low inflation, not only would price stability be achieved, but wages would be forced to adjust to downward pressure, unions would no longer be needed to help contain inflation, and the terms of the employment contract would shift dramatically.

This describes what eventually happened throughout the capitalist world. In the UK the reversals started within four years of the 1975 Employment Protection Act, which had seen the main advances in rights. However, the sequencing of events is more complex than this implies. Not only did such rights as those for women and various minorities start to develop fully *after* the neoliberal turn, but other more general rights (for example, to consultation, to limitations on working hours) were being spread across Europe as a result of the developing social policy of the European Union. Also, as the countries of Central and Eastern Europe (CEE) joined the EU following the collapse of the state socialist system across the region, employee rights spread even further. New member states were required to adopt the *acquis communautaire*, the sum of all current EU policy measures and legislation. Emerging from the different approaches to worker rights of the Soviet system, the new member states rapidly acquired a typical Western European approach to the employment contract.

Outside the UK and the US, major moves against the achievements of the 1970s did not start in earnest until the 1990s. A landmark in changing policy was an OECD report published in 1994, *The Jobs Study*. This tried to demonstrate that unemployment was rising in countries with strong job protection rights but going down in those with very weak rights – mainly the neoliberal economies of the UK and the US. Employment in post-industrial economies, it argued, was dependent on labour flexibility, implying a return of power over labour to employers. Flexibility became the key word in employment policy debates from that time onwards. It had major influence on the European Commission and several individual governments, including those in CEE.

Ambiguities of the Employment Contract

Two contradictory developments – strengthening some kinds of worker rights and weakening others – have therefore proceeded simultaneously, particularly in Europe.

The drivers of change

The expansion of employee rights was driven first, in the 1970s, by worker protests and strikes and later both by separate campaigns for rights of women and other social identities and by the generalization of social policy across Europe by the EU. Different factors have been driving the opposite changes in contemporary employment practices that are reducing the security of most workers. We shall here concentrate on the three main ones: the shift in risk-bearing in contemporary forms of capitalism, the rise of the services economy, and the role of information technology.

The shift in risk-bearing in contemporary capitalism

In economic theory, shareholders' profits are the last claim on a firm's earnings. After paying workers, suppliers, bond-holders and others on whose provision of resources the firm's income depends, after taxes have been cleared, and after its products have been offered for sale at a price customers have been willing to pay, shareholders discover what is left for them, the residual of a firm's gross earnings. This is the risk they take, and it is in recognition of this higher level of risk than is faced by all other interests in the firm that shareholders are able to extract the highest rewards of all when a firm is successful. Risk-taking justifies the inequalities that result from capitalist activity.

In recent years this has changed. Successful political pressures for the deregulation of international capital movements have given finance a freedom and flexibility not enjoyed by labour and other factors of production. At least until this freedom brought us the financial crisis of 2007–8, governments in most countries were eager to attract this free-floating capital and adopted forms of financial governance that favoured its interests. Capital is highly mobile, while states, working populations and firms with committed plant and equipment remain grounded in their territories. There are limits to this mobility. Governments could combine together to defend their interests, though they have strong temptations to play 'beggar my neighbour'. Workers could migrate, though this is far more difficult than a bank switching funds around the world. Firms with factories, shops and offices could relocate, though larger ones can usually achieve more flexibility by themselves developing an international financial arm. The party to an arrangement that can most easily defect and go elsewhere usually has the upper hand. This has increasingly become the case for finance capital.

One consequence of this shift in the balance of power has been the contemporary corporate governance regime, which identifies the maximization of shareholders' interests as the sole goal of a company (for some critical evaluations of this process, see Driver and Thompson 2018). This has fundamentally changed the ideas of profit as a residual. If share values drop below expectations, firms face takeover bids from groups who believe that they can manage the firm in a way that will deliver higher profits. Senior executives must deliver a certain level of profit or face very severe consequences. Profits are therefore no longer a residual but have to reach guaranteed levels; achieving these targets has become *de facto* the *first* charge on a firm. Risk-bearing shifts away from shareholders. One of the key objectives of this turn in corporate governance was to ensure that senior managers followed shareholders' interests. Linking their own remuneration to profit levels was seen as key to this, though there is considerable evidence that the pay of senior executives in large corporations continues to rise even when profits decline (Reiff 2013).

Thanks to the development of increasingly sophisticated forms of risk-sharing through complex financial products in virtually unregulated secondary and derivatives markets, financial activities have become the most profitable forms of economic activity. Making money just by dealing in money, cutting out the middle activities of making goods or providing services that are sold for profit, has become the most rational form of economic action. For firms in other sectors of the economy this presents a strong incentive, first to acquire a financial arm and then to concentrate expertise and strategic effort in that arm. Many smart corporations aspire to become primarily financial enterprises, with other activities, including original core business functions and mass customer relations, being contracted out in various ways (Fligstein and Shin 2007; Krippner 2012; van der Zwan 2014).

Elsewhere I have explored the negative implications of these changes for customers (Crouch 2018), but the burden falls mainly on workers and suppliers (Grimshaw et al. 2006; Lin 2016). Wages have become the new residual (Baccaro and Howell 2017; see also Appay 2010; Da Costa and Rehfeldt

2010; Mésini 2010). The gig and other forms of precariousness are perfect vehicles for this transfer of risk, but they are by no means the only ones. For example, the tendency of much contemporary training policy is for skill acquisition to become primarily the responsibility of workers, who are expected to anticipate the kinds of skill that might be needed by the economy in several years' time (Crouch et al. 1999; Sol 2008). There is a similar implication in the shift of most corporate and occupational pension schemes from defined benefits to defined contributions (Ebbinghaus and Whiteside 2012; van het Kaar 2008).

We can also identify a difference between market and corporate forms of neoliberalism. Advocates of the former insist on trying to achieve perfect markets; the latter defend the role of oligopolistic corporations and therefore dilute the importance of the market (Bork [1978] 1993; Posner 2001; for a full account of how this occurred, see Crouch 2011: ch. 3). Workers' interests have rarely been considered in these debates, though the implications for them are important and paradoxical. Market neoliberalism sees only the myth of an equal contract between employer and employee, while acceptance of the dominance of the managerial corporation makes it easier to understand the 'master–servant' relationship that features in much labour law. This tension within contemporary capitalism can be eased by pushing workers' interests right outside the corporation, the most extreme form of which is the redefinition of them as not being employees at all: the gig.

The complexity of the services economy

The idea of standard employment was very much the creature of the large-scale factories and offices associated with manufacturing and their use of continuous, repetitive work operations that needed to be brought together in large locations. Change has come with the replacement of employment in industry by that in certain kinds of services. Much employment in services activities takes place in very different work environments, with far more flexibility in organization, rates of staff deployment, diversity of locations and, within private services, on the whole a wider income dispersion than manufacturing (Vaughan-Whitehead 2011). Quite apart from the changes in forms of work themselves, the mere fact of the massive differences involved in the shift from manufacturing to services has brought upheaval to many workers' lives, many of whom have seen whole industries collapse in which they believed they had found secure careers. This has created a hopeless situation for those forms of job protection that assume the stable survival of particular firms and occupations.

It is misleading to speak of the 'services sector' either in the singular or as a single tertiary sector in contrast to a primary, extractive (mining, agriculture, fishing) sector and a secondary, productive (manufacturing, construction, utilities) sector. Services are a very heterogeneous set of activities. It is also misleading to see them all as distinctly 'modern', as activities that are concerned with neither extraction nor manufacturing have been important in all societies, ranging from priests to cleaners. To point to the services sectors as particularly relevant to precariousness is not to say that other sectors present no such issues. Agriculture has always been the source of highly precarious work and continues to be so, which is why in wealthy countries it is increasingly the preserve of immigrants, including illegal ones. There are also many temporary and other insecure workers in construction and some in manufacturing. But these activities are declining as sources of employment, while services are growing.

Ambiguities of the Employment Contract

The impact of information technology
There is a major debate over whether information technology and, even more so, artificial intelligence threaten the future of work. Until now, advances in technology have tended to create occupations as much as they have destroyed them. Whether this is now changing will be discussed in the final chapter. We here concentrate on the growth of platforms, as these constitute the challenge to standard employment represented by the gig and some other forms of precariousness. At the centre stands a site on the Internet known as a platform. The platform is owned by a corporation, which is fully protected by intellectual copyright. Nick Srnicek (2017) has compared this sector to extractive activities; instead of mining a mineral, firms mine data.

As in minerals, it is characteristic of platform firms that a small number of them dominate markets. This happens for the following important reason. A platform gives access to networks – of persons to perform work, of products to sell, of technologies to use. A user of a platform normally wants the biggest possible one; few people are likely deliberately to choose the tenth largest supplier of taxis in their city or the twentieth largest online supplier of books. There are therefore strong trends towards domination of platforms by a very small number of corporations. The technical term that economists use for this process is 'network externality'. This process helps explain how it happened that the Internet became very rapidly dominated by a handful of firms with global reach and extraordinary share values, quickly overtaking corporations in other sectors of the economy that had been in operation for many years. Following the Internet itself come the platform firms that use it, where similar monopolies are being established. Where monopoly (or at least highly restricted competition) is a feasible prize, corporations can afford to run at a loss for several years, laying down their networks and pricing so low that they drive out smaller competitors, until the prize of network dominance is gained and prices can move upwards accordingly. This process affects many interests – suppliers, smaller firms and customers – as well as workers. In this book our focus is on the last, but it is important to keep in mind the broader economic processes at stake in this new area of the capitalist economy, an area in which the market itself gradually weakens.

The best-known examples of platform economies to date are those for taxi services, food and parcel delivery, and bed and breakfast accommodation. In the first of these a firm – the best-known names in the Western world are Uber and Lyft – establishes a platform that links workers with cars wanting to offer lifts for payment with customers seeking rides. The customer pays the platform, which passes on a proportion of the payment to the driver. The platform firms maintain that they are not employers of the drivers, just the providers of an Internet app that enables drivers and customers to contact each other. Drivers have no contract of employment and therefore no rights to sick pay, holiday pay, pensions, health and safety protection, or training. They are of course required to have a driving licence, but none of the special professional driving and route-knowledge skills associated with traditional taxi drivers. They are required, like any other driver, to have accident insurance, but no special health and safety protection. In exchange they can, in principle, work whatever hours they like, and they are not subject to some of the disciplinary provisions that affect employees. (They may, for example, ask a friend or relation to do the work for them if they so choose, that person accepting any risk involved if (s)he does not have a driving licence or insurance cover.) On the other hand, they have to maintain a certain level of customer ratings, must usually work to hours required by the platform, and must accept its prices. They lack many of the freedoms of true self-employment.

Ambiguities of the Employment Contract

Food delivery firms such as Deliveroo, Just Eat, Hero, Takeaway.com, Amazon Restaurants, Uber Eats and Foodora operate on a similar basis, though, since the normal form of transport is a bicycle, there is less regulatory cover. In most countries there are no rules governing what cyclists can carry in the sacks on their backs, and if a rider falls off his or her bike under the weight of the load of food, then the resulting injuries, damage to bike and to any third persons involved are the liability of the rider. All the platform firm did, it would argue, was to provide the sack and the app link. It has no responsibilities at all towards the rider, even though the sacks bear the firm's logo.

Bed-and-breakfast booking services such as Airbnb are slightly different. The platform firm provides an app that enables people wanting to rent out rooms on a short-term basis to be put into contact with people wanting to hire rooms for short stays. Labour services are only part of what is being traded here, the rest comprising the rent of floor space. Serious objections can be raised to Airbnb; originally seen as enabling 'sharing' by masses of ordinary individuals, it is increasingly enabling large corporations to buy up large parts of tourist cities for short-term letting. However, for our present purposes there does not seem to be an alternative model of *employment* that is being displaced by the platform service.

A further aspect of the role of information technology in changing the character of employment relationships is the scope it offers employers for surveillance of remotely located workers. Electronic surveillance of the homes of teleworkers has been going on for several years, pre-dating the arrival of the platform economy. Enter 'telework monitoring' into a search engine and one sees a large number of advertisements for products enabling one to monitor extremely closely the activities of one's employees, offering a level of surveillance going beyond what is possible in a face-to-face workplace. Management can intrude far deeper into the lives of workers in the information age, which for many intensifies the contrast between the precariousness of their own position and the control that can be exercised over them. It is already taken for granted that elite sportspeople have their heart activity rates, diets and other functions constantly monitored with technical devices. Only slightly less intrusive measures are used for even routine jobs. When phoning call centres we have all become accustomed to the initial message which says that all calls are monitored 'for training purposes'. This means that every little delay in responding by the call centre's workers, every slip of the tongue, and of course any expression of sympathy for a caller exasperated by the corporation's behaviour, can be tracked and the employee concerned dealt with. A major extension of such techniques is now taking place in professional forms of employment, in particular in education, health and care services. Managers themselves are included, as they too are workers likely to present moral hazards to the owner.

Some of these developments will be generally welcomed; we might all appreciate having the alcohol levels of surgeons and airline pilots monitored. But there is a literature agonizing over the ethical issues this involves (e.g., Fairweather 1999). How far is it acceptable for our movements to be placed under surveillance? Meanwhile, research reports that monitoring workers in this way certainly improves their performance (Bhave 2014); so we can expect the process to grow and become ever more intrusive, intensifying further the asymmetry of the employment relationship.

Conclusion: the ambiguous trajectory of standard employment

The challenges to the standard employment model are powerful. A longer-term history of economic development that seemed to produce constantly improving terms for workers within the framework of the employment contract is being reversed. The gig – in which the very idea of employment and therefore of any rights at all is dissolved – is just the most extreme form taken by this challenge. At the same time, however, new employment rights are being created and extended. Several observers have seen in this process a growing separation, a dualism, between those who remain on well-protected standard contracts and growing numbers of primarily young and female workers who occupy the precarious positions being produced by the drive to make workers the new residual for the profit-maximizing corporation, by the decline of manufacturing industry whose workers were the spearhead of enriched standard employment, and by the instruments of control placed in the hands of managements by new technology. Other observers, however, also perceive changes in the terms of standard employment itself, implying that the idea of a secure part of the workforce is itself disintegrating.

3

The Rise, Fall and Persistence of Standard Employment

The rights achieved under the enrichment of standard employment can be considered under a number of headings: employment protection, ranging from restrictions on employers' rights to dismiss employees to entitlements to certain kinds of leave and protection against discrimination; representation by trade unions or membership of consultative committees in the firm; and protection of income levels in cases of old age, unemployment, sickness and other factors. Together they constitute means by which employees' dependence on the employer, and therefore the asymmetry of the employment contract, have been reduced. We might also consider welfare state services that enable workers to maintain their living standards outside the terms of their employment, such as education and health. These are fundamental to workers' security but lie beyond our narrow concentration here on employment conditions as such.

The mid-1990s are a good starting point for studying change. This was the period of the OECD *Jobs Study*, when European countries were beginning to imitate the neoliberal reforms to employment rights begun in the UK and the US. In the following account we shall consider those larger OECD member states for which data are available since that time. The purpose of considering a fairly large number of countries is to ensure that we do not make unjustified generalizations about trends based on the experience of one or two cases. As we shall see, there are some overall trends, but with important exceptions. It is not our aim here to try to find groups of countries with shared trajectories, though where there seem to be groups this will be pointed out. Existing classifications of types of welfare state or political economy do not give us a clear guide as to how countries are changing, and identifying new patterns is a task for a different project.

The fate of employment rights

Employment protection

Not all workers benefited from the extensions of labour rights that took place from the 1970s onwards. Firms with fewer than a certain number of employees were usually exempt; workers in sectors without trade unions, and especially immigrants, were often likely to be ignorant of their rights and fearful of trying to exercise them; women in low-level services work were often unable to claim rights (Leschke 2015). This applied *a fortiori* to workers in the shadow and informal economies. The self-employed were also excluded, as they obviously had no employment contract, but their numbers were declining. Much of the relevant legislation assumed the standard employment model of a full-time worker with an indefinite contract with employee status, though the essentially male characteristic of that model was gradually diluted by the inclusion of maternity rights. These points need to be borne in mind when we examine the data.

The OECD collects statistics from its member states on those items of employment protection that concern individual and collective dismissals. The data set covers not just legal provisions but rules agreed in collective bargaining between trade unions and employers or employers' associations and the judgements of courts in individual precedent-setting cases. Various measures are constructed from these data, in particular synthetic indices of the strength of protection for individual employees, additional provisions for collective dismissals, and regulation of temporary employment. The procedure and its outcomes can be challenged. Synthetic indices necessarily involve judgements about the relative importance of different items. Also, the OECD is in no position to assess to what extent firms comply with law and collective agreements. Too much weight should not therefore be placed on the precise scores produced by this exercise. However, over the years the OECD has worked hard to improve its procedures; its work is the only documentation we have on such a scale, and we can use it to look at broad trends over time and differences among countries.

Some major findings are displayed in figure 3.1, which presents statistics for 1995 and for the most recent year for which data have been published, 2013. Countries are displayed in their rank order in 2013.

Figure 3.1a shows national scores for the strength of employment protection in the case of individual

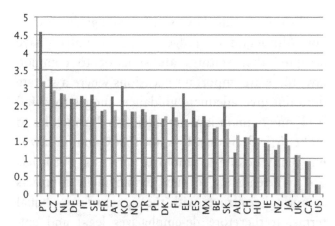

Figure 3.1a Employment protection rights for individual workers, OECD member states, 1995 (dark grey) and 2013 (light grey)

Source: OECD 2018a

dismissals. The overall trend has been downwards, in some cases quite considerably. A few countries bucked that trend in minor ways (e.g., Belgium, Germany), but only New Zealand and in particular Australia saw significant increases in protection, albeit from low bases. There was less diversity among countries by the later date, implying some convergence (primarily downwards). It is notable that in both 1995 and (with the exception of Australia) 2013 the lowest places were occupied by all Anglophone countries. A possible explanation for this is that these countries still use the old

English common law system alongside statute law. Although most judges in these countries have accepted that statutes are superior to common law, there are important occasions where a statute does not give adequate guidance. Judges then fall back on common law precedents and principles to make their decisions. It is not that common law is inherently hostile to employee interests, but it has a strong tendency to view employment contracts as normal contracts with the signatories on equal terms. It therefore de-emphasizes legal and collective bargaining provisions that have sought to compensate employees for the asymmetry of the employment contract. The OECD also collects data on additional employment protection in the case of collective dismissals. There has been some decline in several countries, but increases in a few.

Figure 3.1b presents national scores for the strength of regulation of temporary work. There has been a very major decline in regulations governing temporary work in those countries that had been highly restrictive, offset by increases in protection among many of those that had in the past offered little. The reductions have mainly involved the abolition of provisions trying to discourage the use of temporary labour; the increases have been in the provision of

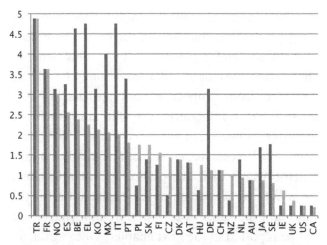

Figure 3.1b Strength of regulation of temporary work, OECD member states, 1995 (dark grey) and 2013 (light grey)

Source: OECD 2018a

rights for temporary workers themselves. There has thus been considerable convergence. The overall tendency has been for temporary employment to be facilitated, perhaps encouraged, and therefore with implicit incentives for employers to substitute temporary for permanent contracts. This has been partly countered by some provision of rights for temporary workers. For example, there are often restrictions on the number of occasions that a temporary contract can be renewed. This can, however, be double-edged; it might lead to an employee being granted permanent status, or it might lead to dismissal and replacement by a new worker. There have also been rules governing the use of employees from temporary work agencies (TWAs), where there is ambiguity over who constitutes the employer. However, in several countries TWAs were illegal until recent years, so their regulation marks a step towards their acceptance as an employment form. We see here some of the explanation for the important increases in temporary employment that will be reported in the next chapter. Once again, all common law countries except for Australia occupy the very lowest positions.

Against this general decline in job protection, various other rights have increased. We shall here highlight what has probably been the most important area of development – around parenthood – though one might also examine the growth of protection against discrimination and other forms of difficulty for women, ethnic and sexual orientation minorities, and disabled people. These are all areas where employees' rights and employers' obligations have increased rather than been rolled back. The OECD calculates the aggregate number of weeks for which mothers have rights to paid maternity leave, both parents to paid parental leave, and fathers to paid father-specific leave. The results for 1995 and 2016 are shown in figure 3.2, ranked by countries' positions in 2016. There is enormous variation, from 164 weeks in the Slovak Republic to nothing at all in the US. Provision became more generous in thirteen countries and remained static in nine. It declined in five, but these were either countries with previously very high provision (Austria, Czechia, Germany) or that saw very small reductions (Denmark, Sweden).

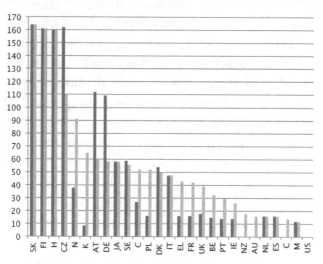

Figure 3.2 Total weeks of paid maternity leave, parental leave and father-specific leave, OECD member states, 1995 (dark grey) and 2016 (light grey)

Source: OECD 2018b

Union representation

Trade union membership, rights and other forms of representation grew during the 1970s and in some countries in the 1980s too. Employment protection legislation usually included the protection of workplace union representatives from reprisals by management. Where they did not already exist, employees' rights to join unions were protected, and in some cases obligations were imposed on employers to recognize unions. The 1970s also saw a considerable strengthening of the powers of works councils and similar institutions in France, Germany, Italy and the Netherlands. Attempts to achieve something similar in the UK failed, and there were no such developments in the other Anglophone countries. An important EU initiative during the early 1990s was legislation requiring the establishment of elected employee bodies, known as European works councils, in all large firms employing workers in more than one European country. Taken together, these developments marked further reductions in the asymmetry of employment contracts, though their substantive importance depended on the actual power of unions and the capacity of workers to make use of them. There were also the usual exceptions for workers in small companies and the shadow economy, the self-employed, and those too weak to exercise rights.

Workers can be represented by unions in two ways. They can become members, in which case their subscriptions and willingness to count as a supporter of the union contribute respectively to the union's financial and human strength. In exchange they can usually get advice and help from the union, including representation over individual grievances. Second, whether workers are members or not, they can benefit from any collective agreements achieved by unions in the firms or sectors in which they are employed. The extent of membership tells us something about the autonomous strength of unions, while the coverage of collective agreements tells us of the reach that unions have achieved in the workforce.

As figure 3.3 shows, membership has been in decline since at least 1995 in nearly all countries except Belgium and Spain. Decline has been marginal in Italy and (from an extremely low initial level) in France. It has been particularly strong in the CEE countries, where it had been artificially high in the early years after the collapse of state socialism, as unions temporarily inherited the formerly compulsory membership of the old state-sponsored unions. Union density remains highest in the Nordic countries.

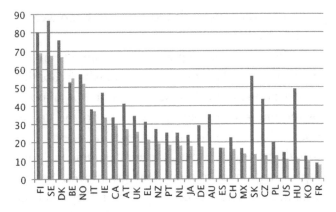

Figure 3.3 Trade union membership density, OECD member states, 1995 (dark grey) and 2013 (light grey)

Source: Visser 2015

It is usual to express union membership as a proportion of employees, because these are the workers whom unions seek to represent, but the total workforce also includes the self-employed and people in the shadow economy. As we shall learn in the following chapter, the shadow economy seems to have been declining in most countries, and self-employment has a varied record. The overall effect of these changes would be slightly to reduce the impact of the downturn in union membership.

Figure 3.4 shows the changes that have taken place in the coverage of negotiated union agreements since 1995. Overall levels are far higher than

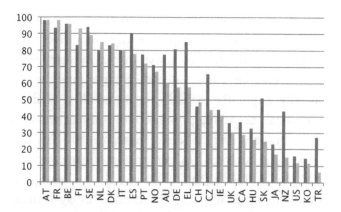

Figure 3.4 Collective bargaining coverage, OECD member states 1995 (dark grey) and 2013 (light grey)

Source: Visser 2015

for membership, and in seven countries there has been stability or actual growth in coverage despite the drop in membership. However, the picture in the majority is of decline, though more than half the workforce remains covered by agreements in twelve countries.

The reality of decline is considerably greater than these statistics suggest. As Baccaro and Howell (2017: 34–6), Emmenegger (2014), and Keune and Galgóczi (2006) have pointed out, data on collective agreement coverage are becoming unreliable guides to the protection being afforded to workers. Increasingly agreements include 'opening clauses', enabling individual employers to reach agreements with company-level employee representatives that offer terms inferior to those in the industry-level agreement. In earlier decades bargaining would usually explicitly exclude the possibility of firm-level deals achieving poorer conditions for workers than branch-level collective agreements. This has now been reversed. In general we must conclude that, with the virtually universal weakening in union membership, the diminution in agreement coverage in many countries, and the growing role of opening clauses in probably a majority of cases, the protection being offered to workers by autonomous representation of their interests is in steep decline.

Income protection, social insurance and non-wage income

The employment contract often establishes both wages or salaries and various so-called fringe benefits, such as pensions and private health insurance. In the free market the levels of these are fixed by the supply and demand for labour. The more that employers want to attract and retain certain kinds of worker, the more generous will be the income and benefits package. These benefits are all in the control of employers and do not constitute reductions in the asymmetry of the employment contract. Where unions are active they might be able to exploit margins available for improvement in these packages and secure better deals than employers would prefer. It is difficult without very detailed research in individual cases to determine whether union power has been operating on these benefits. In estimating their impact on contract asymmetry we therefore cannot advance beyond the input evidence of membership strength and bargaining coverage discussed above.

The situation is different for public policy measures that guarantee workers other sources of income, or of expectations of future income, from outside the labour market. These become supports against the dominance of the employer, because they give employees alternative sources of their standard of living. They therefore need to be taken into account when we examine factors that offset contract asymmetry. In many countries unions have also been represented in the governance of pension schemes, their influence waxing and waning with their general position in the economy (Keune 2018). During the 1960s and 1970s the coverage of social insurance schemes became more generous. In most countries of continental Europe they had originally applied to specific occupational groups, and the self-employed had been routinely excluded. Only in the Scandinavian countries and the UK had schemes been universal. Although employer and employee contributions rose, gradually schemes needed subsidies from general taxation to supplement their funds, diminishing the insurance idea of pooled risks and the rationale for separate funds. Previously excluded groups, such as the self-employed, were gradually included. Women began to acquire rights, though their typically shorter work histories meant that they could usually expect inferior benefits to those of men.

The main constituents of such measures are schemes that protect workers' living standards in the event of employment loss and income-support payments that increase an employee's money income beyond the level that can be achieved in the market. Income loss can result from being too old to work effectively (pensions), unable to find work (unemployment benefit), or disabled by accident or health problems from being able to work (disability, etc., benefits). We shall here consider only pensions and unemployment benefit.

Retirement pensions After the reforms of the 1960s and 1970s the previous automatic association of old age with poverty ceased to be the case in many countries. Important also were reductions in the retirement age. There was a strong rationale for this. In several countries automation was already reducing employment in manufacturing, and it seemed sensible to create job opportunities for young workers by allowing older ones to retire early. This seemed especially appropriate where (as for example in Italy) young generations were considerably better educated than their predecessors; early retirement should help improve productivity. Also, manual work in agriculture, mining and manufacturing was physically hard, and people should not be expected to spend all their adult lives doing it.

This trajectory has changed during the past two decades. Pension reform is today motivated primarily by the reluctance of governments and pension funds to raise taxes and pension contributions adequately to meet the challenges of increased longevity, declining birth rates and more volatile stock markets. In the majority of cases the net result of reform has been to worsen expectations of net replacement rates, especially for workers above mean incomes. On the other hand, improving longevity continues to imply overall increases in pension wealth for individuals. Also, far more women are in paid employment today than in earlier decades, earning their own rights to second-tier pensions.

Systematic comparative data across wealthy capitalist economies have been available only since 2002, which is some way into the major processes of change. These have included raising the age of retirement, reducing benefits, increasing contributions, and changing the basis of calculating entitlements (mainly from definitions of the benefits to be received in relation to occupational earnings to those based on the contributions made by employees during their working lives, making their pensions dependent on the performance of financial markets). The effect of these changes has been mainly, though not entirely, unfavourable to employees' immediate interests – though it can of course be argued that maintaining unsustainable pension levels would not be in their long-term interests.

Figure 3.5 shows changes in the net replacement rates of expected pensions for workers on (a) 50 per cent of mean earnings and (b) mean earnings in 2002 and 2014 (respectively the earliest and most recent dates for which comparable statistics are available). A net replacement rate is the proportion of workers' mean in-work earnings that they can expect to receive after retirement, taking into

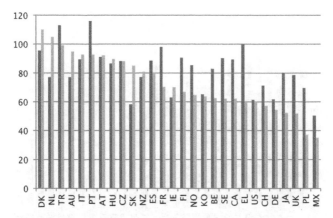

Figure 3.5a Net income replacement rates for statutory and mandatory pensions for persons earning 50 per cent of mean income, 2002 (dark grey) and 2014 (light grey)

Source: OECD 2017a

account taxation arrangements (which are often different for retired persons). These do not represent the pensions actually being received in those years, as these would represent the accumulation of decades of different pension arrangements. For this study we are interested in current policy, which means the expectations embedded in policies for workers just starting their careers. This is what the OECD calculates, and, although it provides notional sums, it gives the best available representation of policy-makers' intentions towards future pensioners. The OECD's data are based on men's

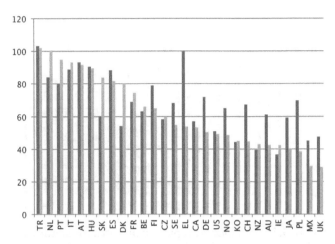

Figure 3.5b Net income replacement rates for statutory and mandatory pensions for persons earning mean income, 2002 (dark grey) and 2014 (light grey)

Source: OECD 2017a

pension replacement rate expectations; those for women in employment are usually the same, but are slightly lower in Australia, Poland, Switzerland and Turkey.

Low-paid workers (i.e., those on 50 per cent of mean earnings) are expected to see worsening pensions in all except nine of twenty-eight countries, those on mean earnings in all except eleven. Replacement rates for low-income earners are typically higher than those for higher paid workers, because the former include basic income support not dependent on income levels.

Unemployment compensation The course of unemployment benefit and various forms of disablement benefit has been similar. An initial period of increased generosity met with sharp reversals as governments in various countries abandoned guaranteeing full employment and therefore wanted to reduce eligibility for benefit in order to lower the burden on public spending. Starting in the UK and the US in the 1980s, but extending generally from the 1990s, pressures increased on unemployed and disabled people to accept whatever jobs were on offer. Often this has been precarious work, leading to increases in the kinds of jobs to be discussed in the next chapter. There was a particularly strong response in Germany, where unification of the west with the state-socialist east brought high unemployment and state debt. Policy-makers responded between 2003 and 2005 with a package known as the Hartz reforms, named after Peter Hartz, the then chief executive of Volkswagen and chairman of the government committee that proposed them. These reforms introduced the possibility of various marginal kinds of employment (Minijobs, Midijobs) and self-employment (IchAG) that unemployed people could be pressured to accept. It thus became hard to qualify for unemployment benefit, the level of which was also reduced.

Social support for unemployed persons varies according to the number of dependants they have and the length of time that they have been without work. It is not possible here to take account of all these variations, so we shall concentrate on families with two working parents and two children, considering their situation in the initial phase of unemployment and then again if still employed after five years. Comparable OECD data do not exist before 2001, and it is not possible to determine on a general basis any changes occurring before then. Figure 3.6 depicts the situation then and in 2015, using data for those countries in membership of the OECD at both points. Two time points are examined: (a) the rates available at the initial point of unemployment and (b) payments after five years of unemployment.

In 2001, two countries – Germany and Portugal – provided an initial replacement rate of over 91 per cent, though by 2015 that applied only to Portugal. Replacement rates of less than 60 per cent were provided by New Zealand and the UK. There were changes over the period, but in both directions. Overall there was decline, but only a minor one, the

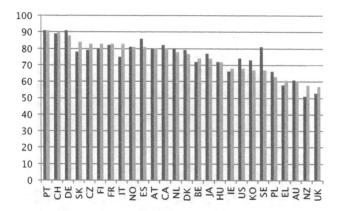

Figure 3.6a Net income replacement rates for initial unemployment benefit, 2001 (dark grey) and 2015 (light grey)

Source: OECD 2016

OECD median moving from 79 per cent to 77 per cent.

Compensation was understandably less generous for the long-term unemployed: in 2001 only Norway offered more than 80 per cent, though Austria, Denmark and Germany had rates of 70 per cent or over. By 2015 no country had compensation of 70 per cent or more. Again, there was overall decline in the median, but only a minor one, from 54 per cent to 52 per cent.

In order to receive unemployment benefit, applicants must be judged eligible. It is therefore

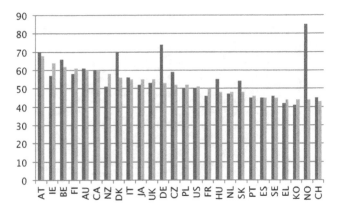

Figure 3.6b Net income replacement rates for unemployment benefit after five years, 2001 (dark grey) and 2015 (light grey)

Source: OECD 2016

necessary to assess the strictness of criteria. This has been attempted for OECD countries by Venn (2012). Summarizing changes in countries between 1997 and 2012, she found evidence of increased toughness in several countries and slight relaxations in very few.

Income support Income protection can also be achieved through measures to support wages for persons in work in order to provide them with a living standard above what they could receive in the market. These take two forms: minimum wage levels that governments require employers to pay and in-work benefits made by governments and paid for out of general taxation to workers on particularly low wages. Unfortunately there have been no major comparative data collections for the latter since 2005, which is too long ago to be useful for our purposes. In any case, minimum wages impinge on employer power in the contract more than state in-work income subsidies, which may actually enable employers to pay lower wages than the market would strictly require. Statutory minimum wage schemes did not figure strongly in much 1970s policy. These were mainly seen as evidence of union weakness, and the period was one of union strength. An important exception to this was France, where unions had long been weak in collective bargaining. A basic minimum wage policy instituted after the Second World War was replaced in 1970 by one that guaranteed the low paid a share in economic growth.

Figure 3.7 shows the development of minimum wages since 1995. It is notable that Austria and the Nordic countries still have no minimum wage legislation. These are countries with particularly strong collective bargaining, and unions argue that a statutory minimum wage would interfere with their work. This has not, however, been the position of

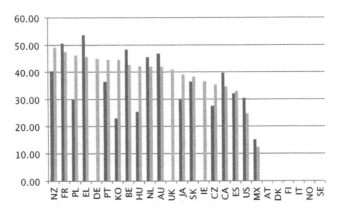

Figure 3.7 Statutory minimum wages as percentage of mean full-time wages, 1995 (dark grey) and 2016 (light grey)

Source: OECD 2017b

Belgian unions, Belgium being the other country with very strong bargaining. In three countries where unions previously took this view – Germany, Ireland and the UK – unions have taken note of their declining bargaining power and have supported the introduction of statutory minimum wages at some point after 1995. Partly because of the dramatic impact of their introduction in these three countries and partly because of gradually rising minimum wages in CEE countries, this area of employment policy has seen considerable growth over the past two decades. On the other hand, most countries with long-established minimum wage systems have seen a decline.

The impact of the crisis

The financial crisis of 2007–8 and subsequent eurozone crisis produced twists to the above account. The European Trade Union Institute has recently conducted a survey of the impact of labour market reforms since the 2007–8 crisis in eleven European countries, looking at both changes in public policy and actual unemployment experiences (Theodoropoulou 2018). The countries covered were Czechia, France, Germany, Greece, Ireland, Italy, the Netherlands, Slovakia, Slovenia, Sweden and the UK. Adopting a synthetic measure of labour market insecurity, the author found that, during the initial austerity period (2007–10), insecurity increased most in Greece (by 77 per cent), Italy (by 72 per cent) and the Netherlands (100 per cent). It increased least in Sweden (4 per cent) and Czechia (31 per cent), where it was driven mainly by the cuts in unemployment insurance benefits rather than increases in unemployment risk. Between 2010 and 2013, unemployment risk fell in Czechia, Slovakia, Ireland, Sweden and the UK. The risk of unemployment itself was higher in 2013 than in 2007 in all countries except Germany. Effective unemployment insurance declined between 2010 and 2013 rather than between 2007 and 2010. The only country in which effective unemployment insurance rose after 2010 was the UK, and it remained stable in France. Theodoropoulou also found a continuation of the trend observed above for employment protection to be reduced, though the gap between insiders and outsiders often seemed to have narrowed.

Another study of the immediate post-crisis period, covering all then EU member states, considered measures taken by governments to shield workers from the employment effects (Erhel and Levionnois 2013). It found that the two most widespread measures were, first, reductions in working hours (with reduced pay) to avoid redundancy (a form of partial unemployment) and, second, increased training. In Germany the government formally endorsed this approach to the extent of making up the wages of workers so affected (Spieser 2013). Employers' preferences are complex. Economists' accounts, such as those embodied in the OECD *Jobs Study*, assume that the main concerns of firms when hiring workers are how easily it would be to sack them – rather than how to ensure they can retain them in order to develop their skills and trustworthiness. The latter may, however, often be the case.

Conclusions

We can summarize the changes discussed above as follows.

- There has been an overall decline in job protection laws, which are strongest in Southern Europe and weakest in the Anglophone countries, but against this trend there has been an increase in parental rights and other rights for employees vulnerable to discrimination in many countries.
- There has been a very strong decline in the coverage of union activities and in particular in membership. Union protection is highest in the Nordic countries and some other North-West European cases and lowest in the Anglophone countries and CEE.
- Changes in pension rights have shown little clear trend in either direction. Unemployment protection has been weakened in several countries, but not in all. Both are highest in the Nordic countries, lowest in CEE.

- In several European countries employers and governments demonstrated a continuing concern for labour market stability by retaining workers during the crisis and improving training.

Overall, there has been a decline in the enriched quality of standard employment, especially in the protection that unions can give workers against the asymmetry of the employment contract. With the benefit of hindsight we can see some of the achievements of the 1970s as defensive measures – ultimately futile – to protect a fundamentally challenged form of work rather than as the progressive assertion of workers' organized power. Protecting workers' rights to their existing jobs, especially when (as in Italy) this included the right of reinstatement, assumed a stable world of manufacturing employment where disturbances were conjunctural rather than structural. Increasingly the reality was that those jobs would never come back.

However, the story told in this chapter is not a simple one of decline. The measure of maternity and parental leave rights discussed above stands as a more general indicator of new kinds of rights that have been growing. As Boonstra and Grünell (2008; see also Knegt 2008b) have pointed out, maternity and parental leave rights even restrict employers' control over the hours that employees are expected to work under their employment contracts. On the other hand, we can extend to the majority of countries an important observation made by Davies and Freedland (2007) in their account of changes in British labour law. Rights of this kind are market-enhancing, being accorded to various groups in order to facilitate their participation in the labour market rather than to reduce the asymmetry of the employment contract. This has enabled many neo-liberals to support the advancement of these rights, as they increase the scope of the market. However, such rights share with traditional employment protection being limited to employees with standard contracts. Employers can therefore evade them as they evade traditional rights by avoiding standard employment. This brings us again to the growth of precarious forms of work contract.

4

The Changing Shape of Precariousness

We must now examine the changing shape of work that falls outside the standard pattern. The various forms of precariousness affect only a minority of workers, but it is a minority that is growing in size and, in particular, affects young people. We shall consider the following forms of precarious employment: involuntary part-time work; temporary work; workers 'on their own account' (including the gig economy); and the shadow or at least partly illegal economy. (A more detailed study of the forms being taken by precariousness in Western European economies will be found in Eichhorst and Marx 2015.)

The different forms of precariousness

Involuntary part-time work

Part-time work has increased considerably over the past two decades. However, it is not necessarily precarious, and it has been a major means whereby large numbers of mothers have been able to participate in the labour force. We should count part-time work as precarious only where the rights and entitlements of part-timers are inferior to those on standard contracts, or where workers would prefer to have full-time jobs but cannot find them. This will often be where part-time work provides only a very small number of hours, frequently as a form of zero-hours or on-call contract employment.

OECD statistics are available for the number of part-timers who state that they would prefer to work full-time, whether because they want more hours, or more equal rights, or both. The OECD calls them 'involuntary' part-timers. The data go back only as far as 2000, but they show involuntary part-time work increasing as a proportion of all employment in most countries covered (figure 4.1). In three countries affected by the 2010 eurozone crisis – Greece, Italy and Spain – the increases have been very high. Involuntary part-time working

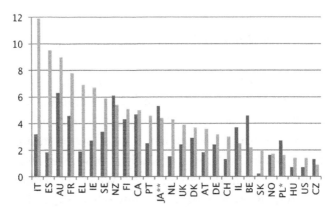

Figure 4.1 'Involuntary' part-time employment as proportion of total employed population, majority of OECD member states, 2000 (dark grey) and 2016 (light grey)

Notes: *2000 statistic is for 2001; **2000 statistic is for 2002
Source: OECD 2018c

now accounts for 5 per cent or more of the total employed workforce in ten of the twenty-six countries covered. Women are more likely than men to be involved in involuntary part-time work and in jobs with very small numbers of hours (Diekhoff et al. 2015; Leschke 2015).

Temporary employment

Temporary employment offers a worker only a limited period, usually a set number of years, of secure work, such employees usually being denied many of the rights enjoyed by those with permanent or at least open-ended jobs, such as protection from unfair dismissal and redundancy compensation. Figure 4.2 shows changes in the proportion of the employed population in fixed-term or temporary contracts in 1995 and 2016. Most of the twenty-four countries reporting saw increases.

Workers 'on their own account'

There are two different kinds of self-employment: on the one hand, small-scale entrepreneurs and

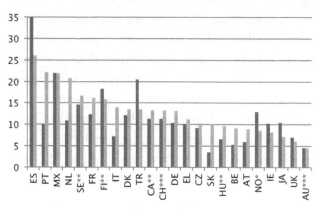

Figure 4.2 Proportion of workers on temporary contracts, 1995 (dark grey) and 2016 (light grey)

Notes: * 1995 statistic is for 1996; ** 1995 statistic is for 1997; *** 1995 statistic is for 1998
Source: OECD 2018c

professional practitioners; on the other, the so-called workers on their own account, piecing together various, usually relatively low-skilled activities. In English law such workers more or less correspond to 'limb b' workers under the Employment Rights Act 1996, discussed in chapter 1. Typically (though by no means always) the former employ their own staff; the latter by definition do not. It is among these that the gig economy is to be found. OECD data on these numbers are published only separately for men and women, as there are often considerable gender differences. Figure 4.3 depicts the changes that have been taking place. Workers on their own account among both genders have been found mainly in less developed economies, where their numbers have been falling fast – spectacularly in the case of Portuguese women. The overall trend among both genders is downwards, but there have been increases for both genders in the Czech and Slovak Republics, Italy, the Netherlands and the UK, very slightly also in Germany and Israel.

The shadow economy

The most insecure form of labour of all comprises illegal workers, those in the shadow economy. Calculations made by the economist Friedrich

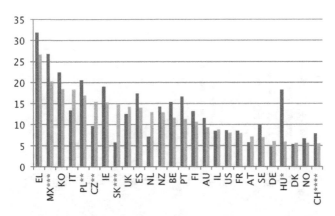

Figure 4.3a Male workers on their own account, 1995 (dark grey) and 2015 (light grey)

Notes: * 1995 statistic is for 1996; ** 1995 statistic is for 1997; *** 1995 statistic is for 1998; **** 1995 statistic is for 2001
Source: OECD 2018c

Schneider (2015), the leading expert in this field, relate to the proportion of GDP likely to be accounted for by illegal or partly illegal activities; it is not possible to estimate employment as such. Given that productivity in the shadow economy is likely to be low, the proportion of workers involved is likely to be somewhat higher. There are enormous variations in its size, which has been particularly large in much of CEE and also in Southern Europe, but according to Schneider's estimates the shadow economy does now seem to be in decline.

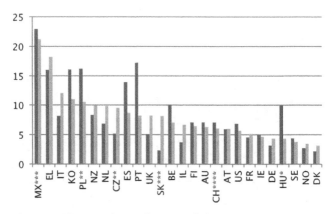

Figure 4.3b Female workers on their own account, 1995 (dark grey) and 2015 (light grey)

Notes: ** 1995 statistic is for 1996; ** 1995 statistic is for 1997; *** 1995 statistic is for 1998; **** 1995 statistic is for 2001
Source: OECD 2018c

The overall pattern of change

If we could add the proportions of the working population in involuntary part-time, temporary, or self-employment and those in the shadow economy, we would have some idea of the total size of precarious employment and how it has changed. Unfortunately, the statistics for the shadow economy date only from 2003 and had to measure its extent by share of GDP rather than persons. It therefore has to be excluded from the account, but it does seem to have declined overall. Since various countries were missing from various data sets, we are left with a reduced group, but it includes the US, the largest European economies, and a reasonable geographical range within Europe. Unfortunately we lose Japan. A summation of the forms of precariousness (apart from the shadow economy) is shown in figure 4.4. (Since the majority of own-account workers is male, the data for men have been used for this item.) A majority of countries show overall increases in precarious employment, and it now accounts for more than a quarter of employment in a majority of cases. This figure would be somewhat

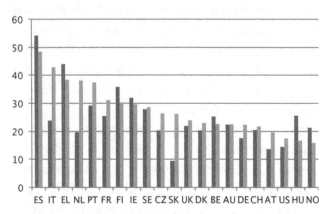

Figure 4.4 Total non-standard employment (excluding shadow economy), certain OECD member states, c. 1995 (dark grey) and c. 2015 (light grey)

higher if we could take account of the shadow economy.

Over time, 'traditional' forms of precariousness – those working on their own account and in the shadow economy – have been declining, a kind of modernization effect as economies have moved out of agriculture and older forms of services. In contrast, types of involuntary part-time and temporary work have been rising. These are the 'modern' forms of precariousness, and they are responsible for considerable insecurity and uncertainty in people's lives, preventing them from planning their and their families' futures. But there are exceptions. Against the historical trend, working on one's own account among both men and women (including the gig) has increased in two heavily industrialized CEE countries (the Czech and Slovak Republics), two highly post-industrial ones (the Netherlands and the UK), and Italy, a heterogeneous economy.

In Greece and Hungary the numbers of traditional workers on their own account declined enough completely to offset the rise in involuntary part-timers and temporary workers. In Belgium a rise in temporary workers was sufficiently offset by reductions in both workers on their own account and involuntary part-timers. In Finland, Ireland,

Norway and Spain, increases in involuntary part-time work were offset by reductions in temporary work and self-employment without employees. Among the countries showing net increases there was also a variety of patterns. In Austria, Denmark, Germany, Italy, the Netherlands and Slovakia, most forms of non-standard work (except the shadow economy) rose; in France, Portugal, Sweden, Switzerland and the US, there were increases in both involuntary part-time and temporary work but not in those working on their own account; in the UK it was the other way round. In Czechia there were increases in both those working on their own account and those in temporary work.

A new labour market dualism?

A key argument of neoliberal labour market reformers in the 1990s was that job protection rights created unemployment, on the grounds that, if employers could not easily sack workers, they would be reluctant to employ them in the first place. Empirical evidence on the issue has been mixed (see, for example, Avdagic 2015). The OECD now concedes that research findings are ambiguous (OECD 2013: ch. 2) and argues that employers are likely to be preoccupied with ease of dismissal only during recessions. (It then concedes that dismissed workers will be less likely to find new positions during recessions, leading to a need for social policy to assist them in various ways.)

The basic unemployment argument also became outdated as firms found ways of employing workers outside the frame of standard employment, leading to arguments that a 'race to the bottom' in labour standards was necessary if jobs were to be created. This has been contested in research for the European Trade Union Institute by Agnieszka Piasna (2017), who used a comprehensive index of job quality to consider change in EU member states between 2005 and 2015. She examined wages, forms of employment and job security, working time and work–life balance, working conditions, skills and career development, and collective interest representation. Although she found deterioration on many components in several countries, she also found a strong and positive relationship between the quantity and the quality of jobs.

The neoliberal critique of labour rights may be on stronger ground when pointing to a growing dualism that is increasingly dividing a secure, largely older male workforce, still in enriched standard employment, from those in precarious jobs. The conclusion neoliberals draw is that dualism would not exist if nobody enjoyed employment rights or trade union protection. In other words, if standard employment is itself precarious, no one need occupy a particularly precarious niche. Some commentators have even seen the growth of dualism as the result of a more or less deliberate strategy of social democratic parties and unions to protect their core, not caring about what happens to the mainly younger workers excluded from its privileges (Rueda 2007). The issue has achieved such importance that in some countries, mainly France and Italy, combating job protection laws has become a necessary symbolic policy for centre-left parties feeling a need to put a 'modernizing' distance between them and their past.

Many unions are certainly falling into a trap, not at all of their own choosing, of representing only workers in standard employment, unwillingly contributing to the marginalization of precarious workers, who might even come to see unions as their enemies (Keune 2015). They usually recognize that this is not at all in their interests, if only because employers can reduce the role of unions by increasing the proportion of workers with contracts (such as those of the gig) that remove them from union jurisdiction (Doellgast et al. 2018). The problem for unions is that, if they can act only on behalf of employees with rights that they can protect, they are unable to recruit from outside that circle and can do nothing for precarious workers. They cannot solve the problem by abandoning standard employees or they would cease to do anything at all.

Unions increasingly understand that they need to learn how to represent the interests and attract the membership of workers in the disaggregated work environments of the digitalized economy, but this is difficult. For example, it means abandoning the tendencies of decades to base their local organizations in large workplaces, partly returning to old methods of town or district organization, but mainly using social media and websites. Much of this is already happening and on a wide scale, but it takes time. (For examples of union struggles among precarious workers in various parts of the world, see the major study by Doellgast et al. 2018; also Thornley et al. 2010; Keune 2015.) Outside the existing unions, new organizations are developing out of the experience of precarious workers themselves (for Europe, see Vandaele 2018; for Japan, Watanabe 2018). These need help and support from existing unions, to whom they can in turn give advice on how to reach the precariat. There is now evidence that unions in several European countries understand these possibilities too. For instance, British unions have been active in bringing and winning legal cases to have gig economy workers accorded some employee rights. (For examples from other European countries, see Vandaele 2018.)

An important perspective on this issue has been offered by Bruno Palier and Kathleen Thelen (2010) in a study of changes in industrial relations, labour rights and welfare policy in France and Germany. Rejecting Rueda's explanation of deliberate social-democratic cynicism, they show how in each of these policy fields governments and employers have produced dualist outcomes without intending to do so. For example, as mentioned in chapter 3, in the aftermath of the 2007–8 crisis, employers in manufacturing secured union agreements to reduce the size of workforces by offering job security to the survivors. This had knock-on effects in social policy, as large numbers of precarious workers were unable to sustain the contributions necessary to admit them to social insurance funds, reducing them to the lower benefits of social assistance.

It is impossible in a project of the current size to conduct a similar study across a wider range of countries, but we can recall the evidence of chapter 3 that governments in several countries have been making it easier for employers to use such devices as temporary employment and on-call work. We can also test some of the assumptions of the dualism theory by comparing the use of temporary employment for the young with the strength of individual job protection. The results of this, for those countries for which we have appropriate data for items, are shown in figure 4.5. There is a modest positive correlation ($r^2 = 0.3112$). This should not be surprising, as the weaker are the security rights possessed by workers the less difference there is between their situation and temporary workers.

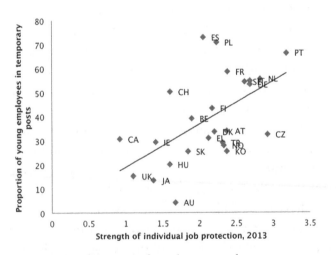

Figure 4.5 Percentage of employees aged twenty to twenty-four in temporary posts (2016) by strength of job protection laws (2013)

Nevertheless, it is difficult to avoid the conclusion that, to a limited extent, job security for some does come at the expense of temporary posts for others – i.e., that there is some dualism.

At the same time, we saw in chapter 3 that many of the enrichments of standard employment are also being eroded. It is not that workers in standard employment remain static while those outside it drift away into precariousness. Both groups of workers are becoming more precarious, while the numbers in the former group are diminishing. Even more complexity is introduced by the fact that, while classic forms of job protection are declining, others, mainly policies that neoliberals themselves have favoured in order to maximize labour market participation, have been growing. Governments have a dilemma. They can hardly disown regulations they have themselves introduced to support mothers in employment or combat ethnic discrimination. On the other hand, they want to respond to employers' demands to place as few restrictions as possible on how they use labour. An obvious if hypocritical solution is to maintain rules governing standard employment but to connive at ways whereby firms can use temporary employment, the gig and other forms of precariousness to evade them. This then produces dualism and exclusion and exposes some of the lowest paid people to levels of insecurity and various forms of difficulty and discrimination from which the more prosperous are protected, even if other aspects of their protection are also being eroded.

5

A New Approach to Employment Security

Two important public policy documents, published fifteen years apart, took different approaches to problems presented by the decline of standard employment: the Supiot report of 2001, prepared by a committee headed by the French labour lawyer Alain Supiot for the European Commission (Supiot 2001; see also Marsden and Stephenson 2001), and the Taylor Review of 2016, produced for the British government by a group led by the public policy specialist Matthew Taylor (Taylor 2016). Both saw the fragmentation of employment as producing challenges for existing legal forms, but they stressed different issues.

Supiot saw that the dominance of standard employment concepts in labour law made it difficult to meet the needs of people outside it, including not just precarious workers but also parents, whose social contribution was looking after their children, or people engaged in unpaid caring. Taylor's brief was limited to the issue of the gig economy. His report saw the precariousness of the gig as a benign development (one of its members had been an initial sponsor of Deliveroo, but the committee contained no worker representatives). However, it was concerned that workers should enter it with their eyes open. For example, it wanted such work to be known as 'dependent contracting', avoiding giving people the misleading sense of independence implied by calling them self-employed, and it also advocated important safeguards of the rights of these dependent contractors. (The proposed Directive on Transparent and Predictable Working Conditions of the European Commission (2017), aimed mainly at helping workers on zero-hours or on-call contracts, is similarly concerned principally with providing information to workers with some very limited substantive rights.)

The title of the Taylor Review was *Good Work*. It did not, however, address two features of the gig that are unlikely ever to be 'good'. First, firms engaging labour in this and other precarious forms of work have hardly any incentive to improve workers' skills or make use of their accumulating experience. For that reason it remains low productivity work. Second, unless Taylor was envisaging an eventual total domination of dependent contracting over standard employment, he failed to see the problems being created by dualism and exclusion, especially affecting a young generation likely to become trapped in insecurity, unable to advance their skills or to enter markets for housing and other expensive forms of consumption except through growing debt.

The Supiot report had a wider ambition. Supiot was concerned that labour law ignored unpaid work and pushed many new forms of contingent employment into a twilight zone. He therefore called for a concept of 'occupational status' (*état professionnel*), analogous to the idea of citizenship in civil society (*état civil*) and extending beyond market activity to embrace other kinds of work and the important transitions between them, as well as in and out of periods of unemployment and retraining. (For rich accounts of the importance of managing labour market transitions, see Schmid 2006, 2015; Schmid and Gazier 2002; on the implications of employment contracts for training, see Busemeyer and Thelen 2015; Sol 2008.) For Supiot, this approach implied a system of social 'special drawing rights', so that people would retain a right to income and other advantages when engaged in socially recognized non-market activities. By making workers' employment rights less dependent upon their current jobs, such changes would spread the risks of short-term and uncertain employment more widely, making them more acceptable to workers. For example, women (if writing today he would probably have added men) withdrawing from the labour market for parenting purposes should be guaranteed a continuous income – a proposal that eventually became implemented in a minor way in several European countries in the form of paid parental leave.

Supiot's view of the 'independence' of workers was very different from that implied by most accounts of the new self-employment. Anticipating developments in Danish and other Nordic work organizations (Kristensen and Lilja 2011), Supiot argued that the most productive and efficient new types of organization were no longer based on the standard employment idea of the work of obedient subordinates. Rather, businesses needed to be able to benefit from the creativity of working people, which implied some autonomy from managerial control. In legal terms, such workers no longer had a duty to follow given instructions; instead, they were to achieve given results, using their ingenuity. Meanwhile the classic self-employed, in most of

A New Approach to Employment Security

Europe found mainly in agriculture, were becoming dominated by strong production pressures from the corporations they supplied. The rise of the 'fictional employee' wielding considerable autonomy was matched by 'the fictional self-employed person', who was really a subordinate. Supiot was writing before the rise of the gig and similar forms, but those in the new falsely self-employed occupations in modern services sectors are in a very similar position to his farmers.

Supiot's ideas have fed into the growing stream of interest in basic or citizen's income, which has tended to submerge his important arguments about skilled, trusted, semi-independent employees. A citizen's income would be allocated by the state, funded through taxation (for Supiot, through social insurance), to every citizen, irrespective of whether or not they chose to work. The level of the income should be high enough to maintain a good, basic standard of living, but it was expected that the majority of people would also want to have paid jobs, partly in order to get a better living standard and partly because the majority of people seemed to want to work. Languishing in a policy wilderness for years, the idea has recently gained considerable currency following concerns about the impact on employment of artificial intelligence.

A New Approach to Employment Security

There has been considerable debate over the economic feasibility of basic income, much of which is well summarized in van Parijs (2018), and the issues do not need to be repeated here. There are, however, also political objections. First, it is easy to launch political campaigns against benefits claimants, even those with sickness and disabilities, on the grounds that hard-working wage earners are losing some of their incomes in taxation to enable the idle to spend their days in leisure. This happens even when benefits claimants have to pass strict eligibility tests. It is easy to imagine the political possibilities opened up by a basic income paid to people with no requirement either to seek work or to demonstrate disability. Mobilization hostile to benefits is especially easy to achieve in the case of immigrants. If, on the other hand, immigrants were excluded from coverage, they would end up doing all the jobs that the basic income enabled natives to avoid, producing an even bigger occupational segregation than already exists.

There is a second, more positive, political objection. At its most robust as a claim, citizenship is a system of rights and responsibilities, entitlement to its privileges coming in exchange for the contributions we make to our society. The strongest claim on society that we can make to a right is that society needs us. This tends to be obscured in much abstract discussion of rights. Even if it is possible to argue that a certain right ought to exist, it is difficult to enforce it unless it can be demonstrated that something is lost by denying it. By making entitlement mere existence, the basic income argument tends to obscure this tough, resilient core to claims for citizenship and rights. This would make it again an easy target for critics of all forms of mutual obligation.

These political problems seem fatal to the argument for a basic income, but they do not dispose of the serious problems that the policy is designed to address. Much care work is unrewarded, as are other services that people render to each other outside the framework of the market, and which may well be better performed outside the market. Unpaid care and parental work could be addressed by making them eligible for special social benefit claims capable of providing a decent income or, where the carer is also able to spend some time in paid work, through major tax allowances. There are already precedents for this in carers' allowances. The generosity of such schemes needs to be improved, and people should be able to feel proud to claim them by making them a regular, respected part of social arrangements. A particularly awkward problem is that the great majority of carers are women, who would come under pressure to stay at home earning a small carer's allowance rather than pursuing careers. This in turn raises even bigger issues over whether virtually all work should therefore be remunerated and marketized, leaving no place for voluntary activity. Here we can only signal the importance of debate.

Low pay below the level of a reasonable standard of living can be and frequently is tackled through minimum wage legislation. This, however, brings us to some of the issues at the heart of this study: the imposition of obligations such as the minimum wage on employers is giving them increasing incentives to devise forms of work that free them from such obligations – for example, by deeming those who work for them not to be employees.

The future supply of work

A major reason why basic income has recently acquired prominence is that the development of automation and artificial intelligence is leading many observers to believe that there will eventually not be enough work to go round to employ us all, even precariously.

A New Approach to Employment Security

Economists have usually assumed that human beings will always find things to do for each other and that, if technologies replace some activities, people move on to find other things to do, usually making use of those very technologies. There has been what the Dutch economist Jan Tinbergen (1975) called a 'race' between technology and education, with the latter usually winning, equipping human beings to do new things as technology replaces what they did in the past. It is often objected that this time it is different, because with the growth of artificial intelligence it is highly skilled work that is affected. Is this really so new? It is partly a result of how we retrospectively view those skills that technology replaces. The art of making highly elaborate copies of religious texts that dominated the work of many monks in the centuries before printing seems to us now to have been a mind-numbingly laborious process. But at the time it was one of the most skilled activities in a society where very few could read and write, let alone produce beautiful texts with primitive implements. Much the same could be said of the extraordinary skill and judgement of medieval architects, who had to work out calculations of stresses and strains in materials without the established knowledge that enabled such tasks to become routine, first by using textbooks and then, in the late twentieth century, with the aid of computers. While there is a case for saying that we have rarely equalled the aesthetic achievements of Gothic and Renaissance architecture, the classification of scientifically based engineering standards by no means deskilled the occupation. The list of similar examples can be extended across the centuries.

Rather than skill levels, it is types of work that are affected differentially by technology. In general, tasks that require some quality of face-to-face human interaction to perform them, whether undertaken by psychiatrists or waiters, are likely to be more robust in the face of both the digital challenge and export to developing economies than those requiring either repeated manual operations or intellectual effort without much need for human contact or creativity (Blinder 2009; Blinder and Krueger 2013).

Some observers see both a decline in jobs overall and a polarization creating increased inequality, as technology provides new opportunities for small numbers of highly skilled people and relegates a larger number to low-skilled services work (Autor and Dorn 2013; Autor et al. 2003). Somewhat different conclusions were reached by Frey and Osborne (2013), whose research led them to conclude that the current trend towards labour market polarization would reach an end point, with computerization being confined principally to low-skill and low-wage occupations. Low-skilled workers would reallocate to tasks that were not susceptible to computerization. However, these would be tasks needing creative and social intelligence, requiring workers to acquire relevant skills.

It is clear that we shall be facing considerable upheaval as old jobs are destroyed by technology and new ones created. There is nothing new about this, but previous episodes – such as the initial industrial revolution – were certainly accompanied by considerable distress and conflict. That will be repeated. Also, the speed of change and therefore the repetition of successive waves of shock can be expected to intensify. Digitalization will continue the present trend for information technology to place increasing powers of monitoring, surveillance and control into the hands of the managers of labour. The character of jobs, how they are performed and with what skills, will increasingly be defined by these managements. This trend facilitates the managerial control of so-called non-employees and thus the gig economy. Further, even though we should expect new jobs to replace old ones, there will be prolonged intermediate episodes when there will be surpluses of labour. This will exacerbate the ongoing shift in the balance of power in the employment relationship towards employers and capital. Further, firms in sectors where information technology is part of the core business will continue their current practice of locating themselves fiscally in the most benign jurisdictions. As this technology spreads to more activities and sectors, ever more firms will be able to do this, creating fiscal crises that will make it difficult to sustain welfare states. Digitalization is producing a world of firms that lack a location and do not employ the people who work for them. This breaks long-established assumptions of systems for determining employers' contributions to such non-wage labour costs as pensions and social insurance (van het Kaar 2008).

Avoiding this dystopia means ensuring that human ingenuity can continue to find rewarding things for us all to do through constant advances in skills and education, improving the value added of as many workers as possible in the economy. It also means facilitating employment in those services where a direct person-to-person relationship is required that cannot easily be replaced by a machine. This implies maintaining and expanding many care and educational services, which cannot be provided in the market and require both a continuing strong welfare state and ways of proper remuneration for care work provided within the family. These goals have a problematic relationship to the widely accepted priority placed on achieving as high a proportion of the adult, pre-retirement, non-student population as possible in the labour market, which has tended to mean both the encouragement of precariousness and reductions in corporate taxation in order to make it cheaper for firms to operate and employ labour. But this latter development is making it more difficult to finance the non-market public and voluntary care work that constitutes an important form of work that we continue to need.

Active labour market policy and flexicurity

Within the European Union, attempts to resolve some of these issues has focused on 'flexicurity'. This idea was developed originally to interpret certain labour-market reforms taking place in the 1990s in the Netherlands (Visser and Hemerijck 1997; Wilthagen and Tros 2004). Unions gave up certain forms of employment protection in order both to improve employment levels and to secure forms of protection more appropriate to a globalized, post-industrial economy. The Dutch reforms suggested that changes to regulation rather than its abolition could also have employment-creating consequences. Initial policies addressed the then very low level of female labour force participation in the Netherlands and the role of part-time and agency work, but it was the general concept that provoked wider interest.

Progress was made at a more general level when Per Kongshøj Madsen (2004) described the Danish approach to flexicurity. In Denmark there had been some reduction in the strength of legal job protection but a considerable increase in longstanding policies of high public spending on lifelong learning and active labour market policy (ALMP), as well as generous provision of childcare support and levels of social protection, together with strong trade unions. It seemed that Danish workers were willing to lose formal job protection for a number of reasons. First, there were such good opportunities for reskilling and career change; second, childcare facilitated women's employment; third, unemployment pay was at a high level of earnings replacement, particularly for low wage earners; and, fourth, unions could protect employees from arbitrary dismissal. Furthermore, as several observers had long noted (Olson 1982; Crouch 1993), unions would be more committed to finding solutions to general labour market issues if they played an encompassing role in collective bargaining, preventing them from looking after only their members' immediate interests. This model both established a more generalizable set of issues and, by being similar to but different from the Dutch reforms, showed the possibilities for flexicurity to comprise a compendium of different but related approaches. In terms of our present study, it meant a change in the character of standard employment enrichment, with reduced emphasis on job protection but considerable strengthening of other elements of the worker's side in the employment relationship, also in the interests of improved productivity.

This came at a particularly favourable moment in the development of European integration, when policy-makers were looking for ways in which countries could find their own preferred paths to similar goals, with exchange and sharing of experiences rather than having to conform to a centralized approach – the so-called open method of coordination. There were also attempts to find a constructive compromise between the generally dominant neoliberal drive for reduced labour market protection and the concern of social democrats that workers be protected from extreme labour market uncertainty. Flexicurity seemed to provide this, and it was taken up in the development of a European Employment Strategy.

A New Approach to Employment Security

But various factors combined to dilute this process and throw it off track (Barbier et al. 2009; Burroni and Keune 2011). Part of the Danish story fitted well into the concept of new social risks then becoming dominant in social policy in several countries (Crouch and Keune 2013). This idea, drawing initially on the idea of 'risk society' developed by Ulrich Beck ([1986] 1992), saw a difference between two kinds of risk that were addressed by social policy. First were the 'old' risks that threatened the living standards of the working class of industrial economies: unemployment, sickness, disablement and injury, and survival into lengthy old age. For these people, risks were dangers from which one needed defensive protection through welfare state transfer payments and forms of legal protection of employment rights. The better educated workers of post-industrial society, argued proponents of an idea of 'new social risks' (e.g., Giddens 1994; Taylor-Gooby 2004), could view risks more confidently as opportunities – calculable chances of improvement. They could benefit from education and training opportunities, as well as flexible employment contracts that enabled both themselves and their employers to match working hours to personal and organizational requirements – including in particular arrangements favourable to women's employment. Childcare services formed part of the same concept.

Some advocates of these ideas believed that the new public spending needed to implement them could be traded off against spending and regulation related to the old policies, a cost-neutral transition from the 'old' defensive welfare state of industrial society to a 'new' opportunity-oriented one suited to post-industrialism and a learning economy. This was also highly consistent with the findings of Gøsta Esping-Andersen (1999) that welfare states which included strong direct delivery of services had better employment performance than those that concentrated on transfer payments – a central part of the distinction between the policies associated with new and old risks respectively. An important factor was that the provision of public care services generated jobs for women in particular, while enabling other women to enter other sectors of the economy, boosting overall employment levels. There was an excellent fit between social policy developments, structural change in the economy, the need to increase employment, and the changed position of women. Certain interpretations of flexicurity were part of that fit.

However, the Danish model covered *both* old and new risks: generous unemployment pay replacement and strong trade unions as well as lifelong learning, ALMP and childcare. But the role of the 'old' institutions came to be forgotten in much of the development of the flexicurity idea as it became an EU project. It therefore became possible for Commission documents to continue to advocate flexicurity while much practical EU policy was undermining it (European Commission 2007; Due and Madsen 2008; Lehndorff 2012; Dølvik and Martin 2014; Barbier and Colomb 2015). An increasingly neoliberal approach was taken to wage determination, implying a reduced role for collective bargaining and therefore for unions. EU policy became particularly hostile to coordinated bargaining, even though this had been the bedrock of the success of the Danish and other Nordic systems (Leonardi and Pedersini 2018). Also, little attention was paid to the idea that unemployment pay might need to become more generous. In contrast, 'activation' increasingly came to be interpreted to mean ensuring that people without work had considerably poorer standards of living than those in jobs.

A report for the Commission on the extent to which different countries had pursued the full flexicurity model *à la danoise* ought to have reminded policy-makers of its viability. The report concentrated on four elements (European Commission

2013): flexible and reliable contractual arrangements; availability of lifelong learning; effective
labour market policies; and a modern social security
system, this variable being divided into two separate parts – social protection and the reconciliation
of work and family life. The Nordic countries and
the Netherlands outperformed the rest of Europe,
the only other countries to come close to them on
a number of variables being Austria, Luxembourg
and, to a lesser extent, Germany. Interestingly,
these have also been countries with strong records
of coordinated bargaining and an important role
for unions, particularly Austria. No country with
low or indifferent scores for social partnership
featured at all consistently on the measures of
flexicurity. Denmark, Sweden and the Netherlands
had high relative scores on all components of the
flexicurity model. Further, all these economics were
performing well. There were also some general sta-
tistical relationships between employment relations
variables (union strength, union incorporation and
coordinated bargaining) and flexicurity indicators:
in particular, the availability of flextime to employees, adult participation in education and training,
reductions in long-term unemployment, participation in activation measures, and the generosity of
long- and in particular short-term unemployment

compensation. There was, however, also a strong relationship between the strength of coordinated bargaining and the extent of temporary work among young people, echoing other evidence of a growing dualism.

In addition, the study found that the pursuit of flexicurity had been damaged by the financial crisis, with considerably increased flexibility as workers had to adapt to deteriorating labour markets, without compensating advances in security measures. This was also the case in the flexicurity heartland. Denmark still performed strongly on all elements but on several its position had deteriorated. Sweden's position was less dramatic, though the generosity of its social protection had declined. There was weakening in Finland, while Germany had seen a dramatic downturn in its ability to keep the long-term unemployed out of poverty, though it had also seen a considerable reduction in those at risk of being long-term unemployed.

Extending the scope of good employment

Flexicurity in its strong sense, with ALMP, parental rights combined with unemployment support and strong, integrated unions can provide a win–

win situation for advanced economies. Workers gain protections from the asymmetry of the classic employment relationship while being engaged in high-productivity activities for their firms. It should be the aim of all relevant areas of social policy – industrial relations, labour rights, welfare state – to maximize the possibilities for such an employment regime. But the continuing hold of neoliberal ideology combined with the residualization of labour implied by the shareholder maximization model is leading public policy in most countries in exactly the opposite direction, towards the encouragement of precariousness and the dismantling rather than the reshaping of enriched standard employment. It is urgent that this is changed.

There is a further argument. From the point of view of economic theory, labour is just another commodity; when it is unemployed it is no different from any other piece of unsold stock waiting on a shelf. This approach might work when the workers concerned have no need for stability, such as students, actors between roles, people just wanting a few hours' paid work on a casual basis. It is not adequate when people can find only such work when they are trying to buy, or pay high rent for, a house, or build a family, or equip a home. The commodity 'labour' needs to reproduce and restore

111

itself and to consume. It needs resources on which it can fall back during periods when there is no demand for it. If it ceases to consume confidently, it provokes recessions. When it gets angry it can be troublesome. The more that employers insist on labour being flexible, the more difficult they make it for workers to achieve the stability that much non-working life requires. As Ulrike Mühlberger pointed out in a relatively early study of new forms of insecure work, insecurity becomes a major externality cost of the labour market (Mühlberger 2000). Firms using precarious labour are refusing to accept a share of labour market risks, instead throwing these onto individual workers, where they often have to be shared and paid for by the rest of society, including those firms that continue to be responsible employers.

The changes being wrought by digitalization will intensify the degree of disturbance to their working lives that people face in this way, producing a crisis of stability at least as important as after the depressions of the 1920s and 1930s. It will, however, be increasingly difficult to tackle these problems as was done then through social insurance systems funded partly by employers' contributions. How can this be achieved when firms have no fiscal location in the country where the work takes place and where the workers are not their employees? Indeed, in many cases the main reason why a firm uses self-employment and other forms of work relationship that reduce employer obligations is in order to evade social insurance and various regulations that ease some of the problems of working life. Their profits are increasing at the expense of those firms that both accept obligations as employers and pay taxes. It is necessary to reverse the highly perverse fiscal and regulatory incentives that encourage firms to behave in this way and instead provide them with incentives to follow the path of strong flexicurity.

A 'use of labour' social insurance

The reversal can be achieved by replacing social insurance charges on employers by those on 'users of labour'. This would work in the following way: *all firms and other organizations defined as being users of labour services and coming above a threshold for exemption should be required to make social insurance payments based on the numbers of hours of labour service that they use, irrespective of whether the contract they have with the labour providers concerned is an employment contract and irrespective of the duration of that contract. A number of important remissions of the charge should then be made available to users of labour who are able to demonstrate that they have accepted certain obligations to the labour providers they use and to the wider community on whom they would otherwise be imposing externalities.*

The first step in constructing this new approach is to define the 'use of labour', reconsidering the sharp distinction between dependent employment and self-employment that is embodied in much labour and social insurance law and practice. The key concept needs to become the use that an organization makes of labour rather than its formal relationship to it. There are already precedents for this. If one employs an independent contractor to carry out tasks on premises, one has certain obligations, for example, to maintain a safe working area. A user of labour services is any individual or organization that carries out any of the following money-earning activities in relation to labour services: establishes an employment contract; purchases labour services; or provides and derives earnings from provision of a platform whereby customers and direct providers conduct their relationship. This is a more inclusive definition than that proposed by Prassl and Risak (2016) for defining an employer. The European Commission is considering ways in which the idea of being merely a 'platform' enables firms to distort various commercial practices. This needs to be extended to include labour relations. Meanwhile, the European Court of Justice has ruled, in a case brought to it by Barcelona taxi drivers, that Uber has to conform to EU policies on transport services and cannot claim that it is in the business of providing platforms and not transport (ECJ 2017). Again, the case has no direct implications for labour issues but further suggests that public authorities are beginning to grasp that providing platforms cannot become a means of evading regulation.

Excluded from the definition of a labour user for regulatory purposes should be individuals or organizations that use labour for fewer than a specified sum of person hours in a given year. This is needed in order to exclude individual customers of self-employed persons and very small firms. Deciding the threshold would be a matter of public policy, depending on what was seen as a level necessary to help small employing bodies. Excluded also would be all arrangements with an individual labour provider amounting to less than a specified number of weekly hours over a year. This is designed to exclude the truly self-employed, who need to be defined as having a sufficient number of customers to avoid their dependence on any one or small group of them in order to survive as a going concern. It also excludes small amounts of casual labour provided by students and similar persons not providing the labour as a major part of their subsistence – that part of the gig that is entirely acceptable, provided health and safety responsibilities are included in the contracts. The number of hours established needs to be small enough to ensure that the labour provider is not heavily dependent on the firm or organization concerned but large enough to make it inconvenient for firms to avoid definition as a user of labour services by keeping a large number of persons on contracts with very small numbers of hours.

Provision also needs to be made for persons working for temporary work agencies, where there is ambiguity whether the agency or the organization with which they are placed is the employer. TWAs cannot be allowed to evade the social insurance rules by allocating workers in small enough numbers to come under the size thresholds. A TWA must therefore be defined as the labour user, though it could subcontract elements of the relationship with the workers concerned, on the condition that these contain standards at least as strong as those that the TWA has undertaken to provide in order to secure its remissions.

Remissions of insurance charges

The insurance system needs to recognize and encourage graduated forms of acceptance of responsibilities by labour users for labour providers. An interesting example of such an approach, though not linked to fiscal incentives to accept higher levels of responsibility, is that of the 'worker' as defined in the British Employment Rights Act 1996 and discussed in chapter 1 above. One problem with the British approach is that all an employer achieves by having the casual workers it uses defined as workers is the acquisition of obligations. This is precisely the approach that needs to be reversed. A second step in the development of a new use of labour insurance system is therefore to define criteria for major remissions of the social insurance charges that labour users face.

Users of labour would have their insurance charges reduced if they accepted the following obligations towards their labour providers:

1 *provision of certain basic rights on the lines of the British 'worker' concept;*
2 *provision of a full employment contract containing all mutual obligations of an employment contract as currently defined in law, including protection against unfair dismissal and redundancy compensation;*

117

3 *provision of contracts without time limits;*
4 *guarantees of provision of training and other forms of skill enhancement;*
5 *recognition of and acceptance of bargaining with autonomous membership organizations (trade unions) representing providers of labour services.*

While points 1 and 2 are cumulative, the others could be adopted by firms in various combinations. The tariff of remissions could be made as simple or complex as policy-makers wish. Remissions need to be substantial enough to encourage firms to want to take advantage of them. The aim of policy is to incentivize labour users to move upmarket and provide 'good work', though possibilities for less favourable conditions have to be left open in order to ensure that the net result is not a reduction in employment. Ideally, 'good employers', those accepting extensive obligations towards the providers of its labour services (in this case true employees), would pay a very low insurance charge.

It will be objected that imposing charges on users of precarious labour will discourage firms from providing those downmarket jobs that offer the only possibilities of sustaining many low-skilled people in work. The importance of this can be exaggerated. Firms who are using inferior employment terms merely because of current fiscal and regulatory incentives to do so can be expected to respond immediately to the reversed incentives by becoming good employers. This will especially be the case where temporary contracts are being used solely to avoid obligations. Those just wanting to make use of genuinely casual employment will not be affected, as their workers will come below the hours threshold and remain in the gig and other forms of precarious economy. In recognition of this, workers able to find only marginal work but genuinely available in the labour market for more substantial posts (i.e., not students or retired people) should be eligible for full unemployment benefit while holding marginal jobs below the threshold.

There might still be some net job loss in the short term as firms adjusted to the new situation. Setting the values of remissions of social insurance charges would need to have regard to the likely effect on employment, just as do bodies establishing minimum wages. As more firms took advantage of the remissions to improve the quality of the employment they provided, there would be an overall gain in productivity and in consumer confidence as more people entered the securer forms of employment. This should eventually stimulate demand

and therefore have further beneficial employment effects. A country such as the UK, which is becoming trapped in an equilibrium of providing increasing employment, but only at the cost of insecure terms and therefore of low skills and reduced productivity, should see its skill levels rise.

It will also be objected that firms in the gig and other forms of precarious economy would remove their employment to countries not reforming social insurance in this way. This is a case for agreeing the basic form of such a system across the EU, with scope for variation in the size of levies and exemptions for individual governments. But individual countries adopting such a scheme alone would attract high-quality employment away from countries maintaining social insurance and regulatory systems that offer the current perverse incentives. Further, in today's services-based economies much work has to be provided at the point of use. Social insurance charges levied at the point where the labour is performed would not be vulnerable to capital flight on these grounds.

The new system would reflect the burdens placed on society by forms of labour use that create insecurity, fail to provide for certain basic needs such as sickness compensation and maternity leave, and keep skill levels low. To object to it amounts to arguing that the providers of insecure, low-skilled work should continue to be privileged over high-quality employers.

Individuals' insurance contributions

There also need to be obligations on workers and other individuals: *all adult persons living in a country, irrespective of whether they were in paid work or not, would be required to contribute to the social insurance fund. Their contributions would not be differentiated according to their labour market status (e.g., non-workers would pay as much as workers; self-employed persons would pay the same as employees) but would vary according to income level, whatever forms that income took. (At present many wealthy people are able to define their earnings as capital gains to avoid the higher rates of income tax.) All persons contributing to the fund would be eligible for benefits from it when unemployed, otherwise unavailable for work, retired from work, taking on specified unpaid care responsibilities or other unpaid work generally agreed to be socially desirable, or giving birth to and caring for children up to a certain age. They would also be eligible to participate in free public ALMP programmes in order to change or enhance their skills. The self-employed would be eligible for the same benefits as employees, including access to ALMP programmes on starting and developing small businesses. Immigrants should be included even if they are not citizens, otherwise they would become vulnerable to sinking into the shadow economy and suffering from various forms of social exclusion.*

This approach follows Supiot's argument that not all work takes place in the labour market and recognizes an *état professionnel* extending to unpaid care workers and parents. Paying the tax but not eligible to receive benefits from the fund would be those too rich to work, having someone else provide for them, or refusing to work even if there were reasonable jobs available.

This is the nearest that we should move to a citizen's income: entitlement to receive benefits in exchange for contributions made of various kinds. This would not in itself achieve Standing's (2009) objective of using basic income to enable people to refuse certain kinds of humiliating work, but, in addition to marginal employment not reducing eligibility for unemployment pay, there should be a list of jobs refusal to accept which would not disqualify a person from claiming benefit. For example, most of us would accept that people should not be excluded from claiming benefits because they refused to accept sex work as an occupation. But the list could be extended, though these would need to be jobs that we should have to do without. Given these provisos, there is no reason why conditionality rules requiring claimants to search in good faith for employment should not be maintained.

Size of the insurance fund

Given that all adults and all except the smallest labour-using organizations would be paying into such a fund, contributions should ensure that it is large enough to be self-financing, including the full costs of public ALMP programmes, without drawing on general taxation, provided individuals' contribution rates were as progressive as income tax. Other forms of taxation would then be adjusted to take account of the major contribution made by the new social insurance system.

This would mark a return to true social insurance principles, improve the transparency and legitimacy of the taxation system (it would be a hypothecated tax), and – of growing importance – prevent firms from avoiding contributing to a country's taxation by locating themselves fiscally elsewhere; they would be taxed at the point where the labour they used was performed.

A New Approach to Employment Security

Worker representation

As discussed in chapter 2, the expansion of digital control techniques in recent years has enabled the extensive monitoring of workers, from call-centre operatives to managers. It is impossible to imagine that workers will ever have equivalent means to monitor the conduct of employers and whether they are behaving honestly in relation to those working for them. The overall result of digitalization will therefore be a further expansion in the power of employers over workers, intensifying the asymmetry of the employment contract. Workers at all levels will increasingly need autonomous organizations to represent their interests in a very unequal relationship. Such a need is not met by the wave of new websites giving gig workers advice on their rights. These can help workers passively confronting a situation, but they cannot represent them in attempts to improve that situation, and there is no guarantee of their autonomy. Workers also need a counter to the capacity of large firms and business associations to devise strategies to advance their interests and lobby governments and international agencies on employment issues. Websites will not do that. Only trade unions and similar autonomous representative organizations can do so.

If trade unions did not exist, it would be necessary to invent them to safeguard workers in the digitalized economy. This is why it is important to include union recognition as one of the criteria for remitting labour users' social insurance charges. We need a revitalized trade unionism, but with a different emphasis from that to which we have become accustomed. This is usually seen as being to secure wage rises, which is an odd priority as, if generally successful, it is likely to provoke inflation. Individual and collective grievance handling, an important, non-inflationary but less prominent aspect of unions' work, will become increasingly important with intensified managerial control and diverse forms of labour relations. Equally important is devising strategies to advance workers' collective interests (such as further developing family-friendly work regimes), something that they cannot do as isolated or only informally linked individuals.

Another old practice that will need reviving is for unions to see themselves as interested and expert in their members' professional capacities. This was fundamental to the original craft unions, and even more so to the 'professional associations' representing highly skilled occupations. These latter used to stand aloof from the trade union movement; today they are more fully integrated but, in the process, have lost much of that earlier professional role. If workers of various kinds are to combat the current digitalized spiral into low-trust, low-discretion total monitoring, they will need representatives trying to push the border back and regain the ability of workers to gain trust. Unions can do this by participating in training and by themselves winning increased discretion for the majority of workers, including exercising various forms of professional discipline over the poorly performing.

Critics of the concept of 'post-Fordism' have long pointed out that Fordism, in the sense of detailed managerial control over workers' movements, has only just arrived for teachers, medical practitioners, care workers, lawyers and others in similarly skilled occupations. There are today considerable grounds for solidarity, or at least for sharing a joint priority, on the balance between control and merited trust among working people at all levels of the occupational structure, including managers themselves. How we establish the right to be trusted and therefore not to have our every movement under permanent surveillance will become a major theme of politics in a digital age. It goes beyond working life to include similar problems for citizens in our relations with police and security services. Governments and employers must be expected to be seduced by the possibilities of total surveillance. But they may become sensitive to arguments about the bad morale and resentment produced by monitoring and the serious trade-off that exists between it and the gains that come from trust.

Conclusion: rebalancing the asymmetry of the employment relationship

The employment relationship will always be asymmetrical. If large numbers of people are engaged in work tasks, there must inevitably be decision-makers who establish the most efficient and profitable ways of achieving those tasks and ensure that everyone involved works to that end. This exposes the lie at the heart of the gig economy, the platform firms that tell their workers they are autonomous entrepreneurs while their efforts are in fact very subordinate, heavily monitored parts of a large profit-maximizing machine.

The issue for public policy is how far the asymmetry can be reduced to improve the quality of life of dependent workers without hurting organizational efficiency. For neoliberals the answer is simple: in a free market, management is, *per definitionem*, the shareholders' agent of rational efficiency; thus anything that diminishes its freedom will reduce that efficiency and therefore general welfare. That concept is the main source of current opposition to all regulations, fiscal arrangements and schemes of worker representation that impede managers' total autonomy. But many firms often exist not in pure markets but, rather, as organizations that offer managers scope for discretion. It is possible for them to use that discretion in malign or incompetent ways, and efficiency and welfare will gain from checks and regulations of various kinds, including for our purposes those affecting persons working for the firm. More significant, there are substantial externalities that do not form part of managers' profit-maximizing calculations even when firms are in pure markets. Important examples are the impact on skill levels of different kinds of economic activity and the social effects of insecurity and weak consumption power among workers.

The proposals for a new form of social insurance made here would not abolish distinctions among workers with different kinds of work security. It would be impossible to achieve this without risking an increase in unemployment. What social policy can do is to give the users of labour strong incentives to improve workers' security and skills and to accept the externalities that result from their activities – either by paying high taxes to enable public policy to pick up these externalities or by internalizing them through their own employment practices. At present social insurance and other taxation heap both regulatory and fiscal burdens on the same labour users, enabling others to escape. This must end. The gig and other precarious forms of work can prevail and become major forms of employment only at the expense of grave social costs. A normal, secure family life would become almost possible for large numbers of people; there would be severe deficiencies in skill levels. Capitalism's own need for social reproduction would be severely compromised. Even if precarious employment remains only at its current levels, it is either producing a dangerous dualism within the workforce or bringing standard employment down to levels of insecurity associated with precariousness. Reducing the asymmetry of the employment relationship can in itself improve the efficiency of the economy, as the continuing economic success of economies with strong enriched standard employment shows. There is therefore a desirable win–win equilibrium for good labour standards within a capitalist economy. The trick is to find it, to ensure that taxation and regulation do not provide perverse incentives that frustrate it, and to do so without giving incentives to divide the working population into the secure and the precarious.

References

Appay, B. (2010) '"Precarization" and flexibility in the labour process', in Thornley, C., Jefferys, S., and Appay, B. (eds), *Globalization and Precarious Forms of Production and Employment*. Cheltenham: Edward Elgar, pp. 23–39.

Autor, D., and Dorn, D. (2013) 'The growth of low skill service jobs and the polarization of the US labor market', *American Economic Review*, 103/5: 1553–97.

Autor, D., Levy, F., and Murnane, R. J. (2003) 'The skill content of recent technological change: an empirical exploration', *Quarterly Journal of Economics*, 118/4: 1279–333.

Avdagic, S. (2015) 'Does deregulation work? Reassessing the unemployment effects of employment protection', *British Journal of Industrial Relations*, 53/1: 6–26.

Baccaro, L., and Howell, C. (2017) *Trajectories of Neoliberal Transformation*. Cambridge: Cambridge University Press.

References

Barbier, J.-C. and Colomb, F. (2015) 'The Janus face of EU law: a sociological perspective on European law making and its influence on social policy in the EU', in Barbier, J.-C., Rogowski, R., and Colomb, F. (eds), *The Sustainability of the European Social Model.* Cheltenham, Edward Elgar, pp. 19–43.

Barbier, J.-C., Colomb, F., and Madsen, P. K. (2009) *Flexicurity – An Open Method of Coordination at the National Level?*, Documents de travail du Centre d'Economie de la Sorbonne, 2009.46, Paris: CES.

Beck, U. ([1986] 1992) *Risk Society: Towards a New Modernity.* London: Sage.

Beveridge, W. (1942) *Social Insurance and Allied Services.* London: HMSO.

Bhave, D. P. (2014) 'The invisible eye? Electronic performance monitoring and employee job performance', *Personnel Psychology*, 67/3: 605–35.

Blinder, A. S. (2009) 'How many US jobs might be offshorable?' *World Economics*, 10/2: 41–50.

Blinder, A. S., and Krueger, A. B. (2013) 'Alternative measures of offshorability: a survey approach', *Journal of Labor Economics*, 31/2: S97–S128.

Boonstra, K., and Grünell, M. (2008) 'From breadwinner to employee with care duties: the consequences of a change in paradigm', in Knegt, R. (ed.), *The Employment Contract as an Exclusionary Device.* Antwerp: Intersentia, pp. 101–25.

Bork, R. H. ([1978] 1993) *The Antitrust Paradox: A*

References

Policy at War with Itself. 2nd edn, New York: Free Press.

Burroni, L., and Keune, M. (2011) 'Flexicurity: a conceptual critique', *European Journal of Industrial Relations*, 17/1: 75–91.

Busemeyer, M. B., and Thelen, K. (2015) 'Non-standard employment and systems of skill formation in European countries', in Eichhorst, W., and Marx, P. (eds), *Non-Standard Employment in Post-Industrial Labour Markets*. Cheltenham: Edward Elgar, pp. 401–29.

Crouch, C. (1993) *Industrial Relations and European State Traditions*. Oxford: Oxford University Press.

Crouch, C. (2011) *The Strange Non-Death of Neoliberalism*. Cambridge: Polity.

Crouch, C. (2018) 'The incompatibles: shareholder maximization and consumer sovereignty', in Thompson, G., and Driver, C. (eds), *Corporate Governance in Contention*. Oxford: Oxford University Press, pp. 263–79.

Crouch, C., and Keune, M. (2013) 'The governance of economic uncertainty: beyond the "new social risks" analysis', in Bonoli, G., and Natali, D. (eds), *The Politics of the New Welfare State*. Oxford: Oxford University Press, pp. 45–67.

Crouch, C., Finegold, D., and Sako, M. (1999) *Are Skills the Answer?* Oxford: Oxford University Press.

Da Costa, I., and Rehfeldt, U. (2010) 'Global restructuring of transnational companies: negotiations in

References

the auto industry', in Thornley, C., Jefferys, S., and Appay, B. (eds), *Globalization and Precarious Forms of Production and Employment*. Cheltenham: Edward Elgar, pp. 62–76.

Davies, P., and Freedland, M. (2007) *Towards a Flexible Labour Market*. Oxford: Oxford University Press.

Denham, A. (2018) 'The gig [*sic*] economy is the future and women can lead the charge', *The Telegraph*, 11 April.

Dieckhoff, M., Gash, V., Mertens, A., and Romeu-Gordo, L. (2015) 'Female atypical employment in the service occupations: a comparative study of time trends in Germany and the UK', in Eichhorst, W. and Marx, P. (eds), *Non-Standard Employment in Post-Industrial Labour Markets*. Cheltenham: Edward Elgar, pp. 353–77.

Doellgast, V., Lillie, N., and Pulignano, V. (2018) *Reconstructing Solidarity: Labour Unions, Precarious Work, and the Politics of Institutional Change in Europe*. Oxford: Oxford University Press.

Dølvik, J. E., and Martin, A. (eds) (2014) *European Social Models: From Crisis to Crisis*. Oxford: Oxford University Press.

Driver, C., and Thompson, G. (eds) (2018) *Corporate Governance in Contention*. Oxford: Oxford University Press.

Due, J., and Madsen, J. S. (2008) 'The Danish model of

industrial relations: erosion or renewal?', *Journal of Industrial Relations*, 50/3: 513–29.

Ebbinghaus, B., and Whiteside, N. (2012) 'Shifting responsibilities in Western European pension systems: what future for social models?', *Global Social Policy*, 12/3: 266–82.

ECJ (2017) Court of Justice Case C-434/15, Asociación Profesional Elite Taxi v. Uber Systems Spain SL, 20 December. Luxembourg: ECJ.

Eichhorst, W., and Marx, P. (eds) (2015) *Non-Standard Employment in Post-Industrial Labour Markets*. Cheltenham: Edward Elgar.

Emmenegger, P. (2014) *The Power to Dismiss: Trade Unions and the Regulation of Job Security in Western Europe*. Oxford: Oxford University Press.

Erhel, C., and Levionnois, C. (2013) 'Les politiques de l'emploi et la "grande récession" du XXIe siècle', in Spieser, C., *L'emploi en temps de crise*. Rueil-Malmaison: Éditions Liaisons, pp. 223–42.

Esping-Andersen, G. (1999) *The Social Foundations of Post-Industrial Economies*. Oxford: Oxford University Press.

Eurofound (2015) *European Working Conditions Survey*. Dublin: Eurofound.

European Commission (2007) *Towards Common Principles of Flexicurity: More and Better Jobs through Flexibility and Security*. Luxembourg: Office for Official Publications of the European Communities.

References

European Commission (2013) *Flexicurity in Europe* (Administrative Agreement JRC No. 31962-2010-11 NFP ISP - FLEXICURITY 2): *Final Report*. Luxembourg: Office for Official Publications of the European Communities.

European Commission (2017) 'Proposal for a Directive of the European Parliament and of the Council on transparent and predictable working conditions in the European Union', COM (2017) 797 Final. Brussels: European Commission.

Fairweather, N. B. (1999) 'Surveillance in employment: the case of teleworking', *Journal of Business Ethics*, 22/1: 39–49.

Fligstein, N., and Shin, T. (2007) 'Shareholder value and the transformation of the US economy, 1984–2001', *Sociological Forum*, 22/4: 399–424.

Freedland, M. (2016) 'Introduction – aims, rationale and methodology', in Freedland (ed.), *The Contract of Employment*. Oxford: Oxford University Press, pp. 3–27.

Freedland, M., and Countouris, N. (2008) 'Towards a comparative theory of the contractual construction of personal work relations in Europe', *Industrial Law Journal*, 37/1: 49–74.

Frey, C. B., and Osborne, M. A. (2013) *The Future of Employment: How Susceptible are Jobs to Computerisation?* Oxford: Oxford Martin Programme on Technology and Employment.

References

Giddens, A. (1994) *Beyond Left and Right: The Future of Radical Politics*. Cambridge: Polity.

Grimshaw, D., Marchington, M., and Rubery, J. (2006) 'The blurring of organizational boundaries and the fragmentation of work', in Wood, G., and James, P. (eds), *Institutions, Production, and Working Life*. Oxford: Oxford University Press, pp. 147–66.

Hathaway, I., and Muro, M. (2016) *Tackling the Gig Economy: New Numbers*. Washington, DC: Brookings Institution.

Keune, M. (2015) 'Trade unions, precarious work and dualization in Europe', in Eichhorst, W., and Marx, P. (eds), *Non-Standard Employment in Post-Industrial Labour Markets*. Cheltenham: Edward Elgar, pp. 378–400.

Keune, M. (2018) 'Opportunity or threat? How trade union power and preferences shape occupational pensions', *Social Policy and Administration*, 52/2: 463–76.

Keune, M., and Galgóczi, B. (eds) (2006) *Collective Bargaining on Working Time: Recent European Experiences*. Brussels: European Trade Union Institute.

Knegt, R. (2008a) 'Regulation of labour relations and the development of employment', in Knegt (ed.), *The Employment Contract as an Exclusionary Device*. Antwerp: Intersentia, pp. 13–46.

Knegt, R. (2008b) 'The employment contract as an inclusionary and exclusionary device', in Knegt (ed.),

References

The Employment Contract as an Exclusionary Device.
Antwerp: Intersentia, pp. 185–202.

Korpi, W. (1983) *The Democratic Class Struggle.*
London: Routledge.

Krippner, G. (2012) *Capitalizing on Crisis: The Political
Origins of the Rise of Finance.* Cambridge, MA:
Harvard University Press.

Kristensen, P. H., and Lilja, K. (eds) (2011) *Nordic
Capitalisms and Globalization.* Oxford: Oxford
University Press.

Lehndorff, S. (2012) *A Triumph of Failed Ideas:
European Models of Capitalism in the Crisis.* Brussels:
European Trade Union Institute.

Leonardi, S., and Pedersini, R. (2018) *Multi-Employer
Bargaining under Pressure: Decentralisation Trends
in Five European Countries.* Brussels: European Trade
Union Institute.

Leschke, J. (2015) 'Non-standard employment of women
in service sector occupations: a comparison of European
countries', in Eichhorst, W., and Marx, P. (eds), *Non-
Standard Employment in Post-Industrial Labour
Markets.* Cheltenham: Edward Elgar, pp. 324–52.

Lichtenstein, N. (2010) 'In the age of Wal-Mart: precarious work and authoritarian management in the
global supply chain', in Thornley, C., Jefferys, S., and
Appay, B. (eds), *Globalization and Precarious Forms
of Production and Employment.* Cheltenham: Edward
Elgar, pp. 10–22.

References

Lin, K.-H. (2016) 'The rise of finance and firm employment dynamics', *Organization Science*, 27/4: 972–88.

McKinsey Global Institute (2016) *Independent Work: Choice, Necessity and the Gig Economy*, www.mck insey.com/featured-insights/employment-and-growth/independent-work-choice-necessity-and-the-gig-econo my.

Madsen, P. K. (2004) 'The Danish model of "flexicurity": experiences and lessons', *Transfer*, 10/2: 187–207.

Marsden, D., and Stephenson, H. (eds) (2001) *Labour Law and Social Insurance in the New Economy: A Debate on the Supiot Report*. London: Centre for Economic Performance, LSE.

Mésini, B. (2010) 'Seasonal workers in Mediterranean agriculture: flexibility and insecurity in a sector under pressure', in Thornley, C., Jefferys, S., and Appay, B. (eds), *Globalization and Precarious Forms of Production and Employment*. Cheltenham: Edward Elgar, pp. 98–113.

Morandini, M. C. (2017) 'Who wants to loosen employment protection? Evidence on preferences for labour market deregulation in Italy', *Stato e Mercato*, 111: 421–58.

Mühlberger, U. (2000) *Neue Formen der Beschäftigung: Arbeitsflexibilisierung durch atypische Beschäftigung in Österreich*. Vienna: Baumüller.

OECD (1994) *The Jobs Study*. Paris: OECD.

OECD (2013) *Employment Outlook 2013*. Paris: OECD.

References

OECD (2016) 'Public unemployment spending', https://data.oecd.org/socialexp/public-unemployment-spending.htm.

OECD (2017a) *Pensions at a Glance 2017*. Paris: OECD, www.oecd.org/publications/oecd-pensions-at-a-glance-19991363.htm.

OECD (2017b) 'Real minimum wages', https://stats.oecd.org/Index.aspx?DataSetCode=RMW.

OECD (2018a) 'OECD indicators of employment protection', www.oecd.org/els/emp/oecdindicatorsofemploymentprotection.htm.

OECD (2018b) 'Length of maternity leave, parental leave and paid father-specific leave', http://stats.oecd.org/index.aspx?queryid=54760#.

OECD (2018c) *Employment Database*, www.oecd.org/employment/emp/onlineoecdemploymentdatabase.htm.

Office for National Statistics (2017) *Contracts that Do Not Guarantee a Minimum Number of hours: September 2017*, www.ons.gov.uk/employmentandlabourmarket/peopleinwork/earningsandworkinghours/articles/contractsthatdonotguaranteeaminimumnumberofhours/september2017.

Olson, M. (1982) *The Rise and Decline of Nations*. New Haven, CT: Yale University Press.

Palier, B., and Thelen, K. (2010) 'Institutionalizing dualism: complementarities and change in France and Germany', *Politics and Society*, 38/1: 119–48.

References

Piasna, A. (2017) *'Bad Jobs' Recovery? European Job Quality Index 2005–2015*, Working Paper 2017.06. Brussels: European Trade Union Institute.

Posner, R. A. (2001) *Antitrust Law*. 2nd edn, Chicago: University of Chicago Press.

Prassl, J. (2018) *Humans as a Service: The Promise and Perils of Work in the Gig Economy*. Oxford: Oxford University Press.

Prassl, J., and Risak, M. (2016) 'Uber, Taskrabbit, and Co: platforms as employers? Rethinking the legal analysis of crowdwork', *Comparative Labor Law and Policy Journal*, 37/3: 619–52.

Reiff, M. R. (2013) *Exploitation and Economic Justice in the Liberal Capitalist State*. Oxford: Oxford University Press, ch. 4.

Rueda, D. (2007) *Social Democracy Inside Out: Government Partisanship, Insiders, and Outsiders in Industrialized Democracies*. Oxford: Oxford University Press.

Schmid, G. (2006) 'Social risk management through transitional labour markets', *Socio-Economic Review*, 4/1: 1–32.

Schmid, G. (2015) 'Sharing risks of labour market transitions: towards a system of employment insurance', *British Journal of Industrial Relations*, 53/1: 70–93.

Schmid, G., and Gazier, B. (eds) (2002) *The Dynamics of Full Employment: Social Integration through*

References

Transitional Labour Markets. Cheltenham: Edward Elgar.

Schneider, F. (2015) 'Size and development of the shadow economy of 31 European and 5 other OECD countries from 2003 to 2015: different developments', www.econ.jku.at/members/Schneider/files/publicat ions/2015/ShadEcEurope31.pdf.

Sol, E. (2008) 'The employment contract and vocational training and education', in Knegt, R. (ed.), *The Employment Contract as an Exclusionary Device.* Antwerp: Intersentia, pp. 127–57.

Spieser, C. (ed.) (2013) *L'emploi en temps de crise.* Rueil-Malmaison: Éditions Liaisons.

Srnicek, N. (2017) *Platform Capitalism.* Cambridge: Polity.

Standing, G. (2009) *Work after Globalization.* Cheltenham: Edward Elgar.

Standing, G. (2011) *The Precariat.* London: Bloomsbury.

Steinmetz, K. (2015) 'Why the California ruling on Uber should frighten the sharing economy', *Time*, 17 June 2015.

Supiot, A. (2001) *Beyond Employment: Changes in Work and the Future of Labour Law in Europe.* Oxford: Oxford University Press.

Taylor, M. (2016) *Good Work: The Taylor Review of Modern Working Practices.* London: Department for Business, Energy and Industrial Strategy.

Taylor-Gooby, P. (ed.) (2004) *New Risks, New Welfare:*

References

The Transformation of the European Welfare State. Oxford: Oxford University Press.

Theodoropoulou, S. (2018) *Drifting into Labour Market Insecurity? Labour Market Reforms in Europe after 2010*, Working Paper 2018.3. Brussels: European Trade Union Institute.

Thornley, C., Jefferys, S., and Appay, B. (eds) (2010) *Globalization and Precarious Forms of Production and Employment.* Cheltenham: Edward Elgar.

Tinbergen, J. (1975) *Income Distribution: Analysis and Policies.* Amsterdam: North Holland.

Vandaele, K. (2018) *Will Trade Unions Survive in the Platform Economy? Emerging Patterns of Platform Workers' Collective Voice and Representation in Europe*, Working Paper 2018.05. Brussels: European Trade Union Institute.

van der Zwan, N. (2014) 'Making sense of financialization', *Socio-Economic Review*, 12/1: 99–129.

van het Kaar, R. H. (2008) 'Employment contracts and pensions', in Knegt, R. (ed.), *The Employment Contract as an Exclusionary Device.* Antwerp: Intersentia, pp. 159–84.

van Parijs, P. (ed.) (2018) *Basic Income and the Left.* London: Social Europe.

Vaughan-Whitehead, D. (ed.) (2011) *Work Inequalities in the Crisis: Evidence from Europe.* Cheltenham: Edward Elgar.

Venn, D. (2012) *Eligibility Criteria for Unemployment*

References

Benefits: Quantitative Indicators for OECD and EU Countries, Social, Employment and Migration Working Paper 131. Paris: OECD.

Verhulp, E. (2008) 'The employment contract as a source of concern', in Knegt, R. (ed.), *The Employment Contract as an Exclusionary Device*. Antwerp: Intersentia, pp. 47–73.

Visser, J. (2015) *ICTWSS Data Base, Version 5.0.* Amsterdam: Amsterdam Institute for Advanced Labour Studies (AIAS).

Visser, J., and Hemerijck, A. (1997) *'A Dutch Miracle': Job Growth, Welfare Reform and Corporatism in the Netherlands*. Amsterdam: Amsterdam University Press.

Watanabe, H. R. (2018) 'The political agency and social movements of Japanese individually-affiliated unions', *Economic and Industrial Democracy*, July, https://doi.org/10.1177/0143831X18789794.

Whiteside, N. (2017) 'Flexible employment and casual labour: a historical perspective on labour market policy', www.historyandpolicy.org/policy-papers/papers/flexible-employment-and-casual-labour-a-historical-perspective-on-labour-ma.

Wilthagen, T., and Tros, F. (2004) 'The concept of "flexicurity": a new approach to regulating employment and labour markets', *Transfer*, 10/2: 166–86.